Tales of Los Alamos
Life on the Mesa 1943-1945

Tales of Los Alamos
Life on the Mesa 1943–1945

By Bernice Brode

Los Alamos Historical Society
Los Alamos, New Mexico
1997
Second printing 2006

Library of Congress Cataloging-in-Publication Data

Brode, Bernice.
 Tales of Los Alamos: Life on the Mesa 1943–45/ by Bernice Brode;
 Barbara G. Storms, editor.
   p. cm.
 Includes index.
   ISBN-10: 0-941232-17-4
1. Los Alamos (N.M.)—History—Anecdotes. 2. Nuclear scientist—United States—Social life and customs. 3. Brode, Bernice—Biography. 4. Brode, Bernice—Anecdotes, etc. 5. United States. Army. Corps of Engineers. Manhattan District—History
1. Storms. Barbara G. 11. Title.
QC773.3.U5B76   1997

                                        97-29558

Photo Credits: Los Alamos Historical Society, except photos of 109 East Palace Avenue and Los Alamos Hospital that are courtesy of Los Alamos National Laboratory.

Other Los Alamos Historical Society books on the Manhattan Project include:

Los Alamos: Beginning of an Era 1943–1945
Gatekeeper to Los Alamos by Nancy Cook Steeper
Inside Box 1663 by Eleanor Jette
Life Within Limits by Eleanor Stone Roensch
In August 1945 by Paul Numerof
Standing By and Making Do (Edited by Jane S. Wilson and Charlotte Serber)
Norris Bradbury (Edited by Virginia Ebinger)
Manhattan District History: Nonscientific Aspects of Los Alamos Project Y through 1946
   by Edith C. Truslow for the Los Alamos Scientific Laboratory
Robert Oppenheimer 1904–1967 by Robert F. Bacher
The Secret Project Notebook by Carolyn Reeder (a novel for young readers)
Twilight Time by Ralph C. Sparks

Los Alamos Historical Society
P.O. Box 43
Los Alamos, New Mexico 87544

Second printing 2006
Printed in Canada

Contents

Preface

To most of the world, the atomic age began in 1945 when the first atomic bomb brought an end to World War 11. To a few hundred others it began much earlier—in utmost secrecy in the ramshackle community of Los Alamos, high in the New Mexico mountains, where a specially selected group of people gathered to design and assemble the atomic weapons.

For Bernice Brode, the new age began in the spring of 1943 as J. Robert Oppenheimer appeared at her home to urge her physicist husband, Robert, to join the scientific team headed for Los Alamos and the Manhattan Project. Like most other project wives, she knew nothing about what her husband would be doing, but she recognized that the new assignment was something "not to be missed." Shortly thereafter, the Brodes and their two young sons disappeared onto the isolated mesa for a life of unaccustomed hardships and high adventure.

Bernice paid close attention, took notes and shortly after the end of the war began writing her first-hand account of the strange and secret life at Los Alamos. Her stories are not about the challenging scientific problems to be solved, the pressure of extreme urgency, the hours and days and months of exhausting work. Instead she tells of day-to-day life in wartime isolation—coping with milk rationing, wilted vegetables, Army regulations, water shortages, neighborhood conflicts, and banding together to create home-grown social and cultural activities.

Back home in Berkeley in the 1950's, Bernice worked with magazine publishers who were interested in her stories and made a number of the revisions and additions they requested. But in the end she gave the Los Alamos Scientific Laboratory permission to publish the manuscript. *Tales of Los Alamos* appeared in the Laboratory house organ, *LASL Community News*, in serial form in the summer of 1960 in commemoration of the 15th anniversary of the dawning of the atomic age.

After Bernice died in 1989, her daughter-in-law, Joanne Brode, gave the Los Alamos Historical Society permission to publish *Tales* and donated a wealth of archival material, including some of Bernice's censor-approved wartime correspondence. Because I was editor of the *LASL News* in the '60's, I was asked to put the manuscript into book form, and I became editor, designer and compositor. The manuscript required only light polishing, primarily to bring parts of the wartime stories into the 1990's while maintaining the attitudes and phraseology of the 1940's. We also deemed it appropriate to identify some of the prominent names in the cast of characters and define some terminology of the times and of the region for the benefit of new generations of readers.

For help in this undertaking, I am greatly indebted to many: Hedy Dunn, curator Shelley Morris, and archivist Theresa Strottman, all of the Historical Society, and historian Roger Meade of the Los Alamos National Laboratory for tracking down photographs; artist Elizabeth Fisher for her cover drawings; Virginia Ebinger, B. J. Wood, Marge McCormick and all the other members of the Publications Committee for proofreading, critiques and encouragement; and my son, Steve, who always knew what to do when the computer protested my various efforts. And most of all, of course, the Historical Society is indebted to Joanne Brode for her contributions and her permission.

Barbara Storms, Editor

Introduction

It was wartime Washington early in March of 1943, when our friend J. Robert Oppenheimer came to see us in our chilly living room. Heat was rationed, and our rented house in Chevy Chase was cheerless and damp. But Oppie did not notice. I could see he was burning with an inner fire as he told us about his new war project, to be situated in the desert of New Mexico, 40 miles from Santa Fe, high up on a mesa. I remembered how he once had said that his two loves—physics and desert country—never existed together. Had he joined them at last?

He was vague about everything, but his eyes had that special intensity, peculiar to him, when he said to me, "I think you will like that life up there, Bernice. It will be quite nice, even in wartime." He made it seem like high adventure rather than patriotic duty, and I felt it was not to be missed.

I did not see Oppie again until six months later when we arrived at his Shangri-la. It was called Manhattan District in Washington, Site Y in Santa Fe, and Los Alamos up on the mesa top itself. Anywhere else it was not to be mentioned at all. Our sole address would be P.O. Box 1663, Santa Fe.

In the months after Oppie's visit, my husband Bob had finished his current war project, the proximity fuse, and had begun making mysterious trips to New Mexico while I remained in Washington with our boys, Bill, 12, and Jack, 11. We had been asked not to come to Site Y until September, as the apartment assigned to us had sixteen Wacs living in it, waiting for their new barracks. So we returned to our home in Berkeley, carrying our inner secrets and bursting with anticipation. It was our last summer in the pre-atomic age.

More than two years later in the early afternoon of August 6, 1945, the atomic age was announced to the world by the devastating bomb. My boys and I were boarding a Navy bus in Pasadena to visit the China Lake Naval Weapons Center in California when we read the headlines. Bill, my older boy, said very quietly, "This is Papa's bomb, you know, Mama." My eyes quickly caught the words from the paper: *atomic bomb, Hiroshima, Los Alamos*. The first two I had never heard of, but the last one, the forbidden name we had not dared utter in our letters home for more than two years, was now, incredibly, staring at me from a newspaper. So that was what we were making up there, "the world's most devastating weapon." My heart beat very fast as I tried to read on and collect my wits and the facts.

A lady in front of me asked what an atomic bomb was and what was this place called Los Alamos. I did not know how to answer. Was the ban of secrecy off now? Could I tell that we lived there and were returning there next week? Security had us so well trained after two years of indoctrination, I was unsure. I said simply, "I don't know what an atomic bomb is, but I hope it ends the war as the paper claims."

Jack whispered to me, "Mama, don't you really know about the bomb?" I really did not as I have no scientific training and anything I heard or saw in the sacrosanct Technical Area where I worked meant nothing to me. I only knew we were doing some war work that had to be finished before the Germans could beat us to it.

When we returned to Los Alamos a week later, all the children were calling the new weapon "Papa's bomb" and bragging to each other how much they knew about it all along. The wives were talking excitedly about leaving our ramshackle community and returning to civilian life, and some were already starting back.

Today Los Alamos is a thriving modern and open city. The Los Alamos National Laboratory is one of the most famous of the country's nuclear science research institutions.

But it was not always so.

1 **Arrival**

"The notion of disappearing into the desert for an undetermined period and under quasi-military auspices disturbed a good many scientists and the families of many more—but there was another side to it—"

—From Oppenheimer's letter to the AEC, 1954

I n September 1943 the Brode family set forth in our old Ford to disappear into the desert, to a place not shown on any map. Our first official stop was at 109 East Palace Avenue in Santa Fe, the regional office of the secret Manhattan Project. I was surprised to see a sign over the archway reading "U.S. Army Corps of Engineers," for we had been told that fact in itself was to be unmentionable. A few months later the sign was removed from outside and put over the inner door.

In the street in front of 109, taking up more than its share of the lane, a dilapidated school bus, marked "U.S. Army" in bright paint, was parked. A big soldier was good-naturedly loading his bus with awkward household purchases such as brooms, mops, mirrors, potted plants, and kiddy-cars. He was taking orders from pert little housewives, with toddlers in tow, to "be careful, for goodness sake." This was the bus to Los Alamos, making two round trips a day, morning and afternoon. We parked behind it and watched the scene.

"For cryin' out loud, lady," the soldier was saying, "we got a war on, remember. For this I join the Army!" He threw up his hands in mock despair, but carefully lifted a small, whining boy into the bus. Then he shouted like a circus barker: "Bus leaving for the wilderness up yonder, everybody in! All aboard, hur-ry, hur-ry, hur-ry!" There was another wild scramble with too many children and too many parcels all pushing into the sagging bus. Then the GI fished a length of rope from his pocket, boarded the bus himself and tied the door handle to the front window. As I watched in amazement, he grinned

109 East Palace, under the portal and across a courtyard, became the first stop for new Los Alamos arrivals.

and said, "Lady, the General hisself told me not to lose any of 'em. Seems they're scarce." The rickety bus rattled off with everyone waving good-by to us as if they were off on a picnic.

We went into the courtyard to the shabby screen door leading to the inner office of 109. There my husband introduced us to Dorothy McKibbin, who was in charge not only of the office but of many other things. A lovely, smiling woman with shining hair and a blue tweed outfit to match her eyes, she maintained a quiet grace in the midst of all the hubbub—hostess rather than a charge d'affaires.

"Welcome, Brode family, and do find chairs while I phone to the site that you've arrived," she said. "We'll have a little peace now that the bus has left. Oh dear, I see Mrs. J left her coat. I'll have to remember to send it up on the afternoon bus." She had an air of handling people easily, and only later did I come to know the serious difficulties she had avoided for all of us.

The whole place seemed more like a storeroom than an office. There was a minimum of furniture—two desks and an assortment of old kitchen chairs—with most of the space taken up by stacks of queer-looking crates and bundles of local purchases here, there and

12

Otowi Bridge, spanning the Rio Grande, was considered too fragile to carry trucks and Army buses.

everywhere. I tried not to be too curious, but it was all so different from the red-tape severity of Washington offices. Indeed, it was "quite nice," as Oppenheimer had promised.

Dorothy made out temporary passes for the boys and me as she chatted. "Make this your headquarters when you come to Santa Fe. Everybody does. Leave your parcels here and meet each other here. That's what this office is really for." So 109 East Palace and Dorothy, our only link with Santa Fe, became our private secret club in the capital of New Mexico. There we could talk and make plans and have no fear of being overheard. All newcomers passed through this office and were sent up to Los Alamos with their misgivings replaced by trust in the unknown "up yonder." Dorothy was a happy choice for our introduction to the war years on the Mesa.

That September day we said good-bye to Dorothy and proceeded up the Taos Highway and onto a washboard dirt road. My husband began to sing—a sure sign he was confidently driving his family into something they would enjoy. I was bewitched by the scenery—the stretches of red earth and pink rocks with dark shrubbery scattered along the ochre cliffs; lavender vistas in the distant Sangre de Cristo mountain range. Color was everywhere. Occasionally adobe houses arose from the earth with strings of scarlet chile peppers hung outside to dry. The flat roofs were strung with ears of yellow, blue, white and dark red corn, also drying in the sun. We passed the turnoff for San Ildefonso Pueblo, with its sacred Black Mesa in the distance, and crossed the narrow wooden bridge over the muddy Rio Grande at Otowi ("the place where the river makes a noise").

"Army buses and trucks are not allowed to go over the bridge," Bob announced. "They have to go around the longer road by way of Española." The boys exclaimed that they could see water through the broken planks.

All was beauty and quiet. No sign of the war-torn world had reached these remote parts. What a superb retreat in which to spend the war years, I thought, with a rising feeling of guilt. But the thought came too soon. Around the next curve we met our first Army construction work, and a sense of alarm chased away any sense of guilt. Huge bulldozers were tearing down the beautiful rock cliffs and leveling off everything in their paths. Their GI drivers seemed unnecessarily happy and purposeful about the destructive work. In the next few years I was to learn that the Army would maintain this bulldozing momentum, conquering and leveling mesa after mesa, replacing strata of timeless growth with ugly buildings whose purpose was not beauty but grim utility.

Choking, blinking, and covered with that layer of dust we were to know so intimately in the next years, we arrived at the East

In the fall of 1943, bulldozers were tearing down cliffs and leveling hills to improve the rugged road to Los Alamos.

Gate. Immediately we were surrounded by armed military police who examined our passes carefully, peered into our car without a word, then waved us on through the gate. The next three miles into town were noisy and lively with construction and confusion. You could scarcely see for the dust churned up by vehicles going in all directions.

"The next stop," Bob announced as if he were conducting a tour, "will be the old stone pump house." There it was, a picturesque

The old shingled water tower was the town's favorite landmark.

remnant of the Los Alamos Ranch School, an exclusive school for boys, recently acquired by the Army. Now, amidst deafening noise of a rising war factory, two-story wooden buildings were going up all around it. On a bit of the old flagstone walk outside we encountered Sally (Mrs. Donald "Moll") Flanders, who had a Dutch haircut and a hardy look about her. All in one breath, Sally welcomed us and ordered Bob to bring us all to the square dance that evening in the theater.

Inside the pump house, now the temporary Security Office, businesslike Wacs took our fingerprints and pressed them on the permanent passes that we needed coming and going through the gates. It was soon regarded as a social error to forget one's pass, especially when everyone had to wait while someone went back the six-mile round trip to fetch it. Another Wac photographed us in a makeshift booth. We were asked for any identifying scars or oddities on our person, and these were written on the passes and recorded in the books, rather frightening by implication. Soon we became accustomed to the unusual tests and questions.

Next we went to sign in at the Housing Office in an old wooden garage beside the water tower. Vera (Mrs. John) Williams was in charge, and we could barely greet her in the surrounding madhouse of young people seeking priorities for still-to-be-erected housing units. But Vera was tough and equal to all of it. She laughed and handed us our permision-for-occupancy slip for the apartment Bob had reserved.

Outside again, we paused to look at the round, shingled water tower, on stilts, that marked the center of our town and became the favorite landmark. Streets had no names, and all directions for finding houses were given in relation to the water tower. It assumed a symbolic stature in our lives—a reminder of the quiet pre-atomic days, before the galloping changes came over the Mesa. In winter long icicles hung over the sides to the delight of the small fry who picked them up when they fell melting in the sun. The water tower was also to be the crux of our worst community crisis, the Water Shortage of 1945.

Our Ford turned down the road from the water tower in search of our new home, designated T-124 C. There, at the far end of the slope where the last of the green Army-constructed clapboard houses were arranged on a pleasantly irregular semicircle, was T-124. Robert Oppenheimer had insisted that the houses follow the natural contours of the land rather than the straight-row formation so dear to the hearts of the Army. General Leslie Groves head of the Manhattan District, gave in but he grumbled to Oppie, "All this nonsense because the families have to live here. If I could have my way and put all these scientists in uniform and in barracks, there would be no fuss and feathers." But Groves had to put up with the families—and the fuss and feathers.

Three first memories of my impact with T-124, as we alighted in front of the house, remain sharp in my mind. There was a beautiful remote vista of the Jemez Mountains behind the houses; the confusion of people, mostly children, in the immediate front lower East Side in New York; and an unsightly telephone pole right in the middle of an otherwise attractive open space. This proved more unaccountable as time went on, for we had no phones in any of the houses, and the pole was very much in the way for parking cars or playing baseball. But many things were unaccountable in those days.

Our car was besieged at once by an unofficial welcoming committee from the four or five nearby four-family houses. Some were unknown neighbors come to have a look at the new residents and some were old friends. We were plunged instantly into the intricacies of Mesa life. Jean (Mrs. Robert) Bacher came rushing out to tell us of other mutual friends soon to arrive. Then she broke off abruptly to ask if my boys could baby-sit for her little ones that very night. Alice (Mrs. Cyril) Smith, whom I met for the first time, sounded me out on sharing half of her teaching job in social sciences in the school that hadn't begun yet. Erica (Mrs. Hans) Staub, a tall, dignified Swiss woman, was introduced while trying to pacify little Mutsie, who had fallen in the dust from her swing. Mici (Mrs. Edward) Teller, a Hungarian woman with short black hair and a rather breathless approach to life, decided then and there to have a tea party that afternoon. "I have rescued my pines from the Army yesterday, and now we should celebrate my victory," she gave as the grand reason.

And so it went, everyone full of plans and enthusiasm.

We hadn't, at this point, even gone inside our apartment. All ages of children were chasing each other up the stairs and all over. Barefoot girls were hopping in the dust for hopscotch, a baseball game was going on in the road, housewives were hanging out clothes on lines strung between houses or attached to trees.

It was tall and stately Alice, with her little Anne in tow, who piloted us inside our kitchen door. Her family lived in the other upper half of T-124. Our apartment was furnished in the GI way— "Government issue plain functional," it was officially called—to tide us over until our own van arrived from Berkeley. Alice and Mici had added little niceties, such as good pots and pans, vases of wild flowers, milk in the refrigerator and made-up beds. Only later did I realize what an effort and sacrifice the milk gift had been.

We inspected our new abode, going down the narrow hall to the three small bedrooms, wondering how sixteen Wacs had ever slept there. There was one tiny bath with funny dull black faucets and a cement-and-tile-lined shower. The pleasant living room had a fireplace and a sweeping view over the canyon to the mountains. The dining nook at one end looked down on the road scene we had just left. The kitchen was quite large with two sinks and a lot of cupboards. It was dominated by a huge black wood-burning cooking stove right in the middle of the room "for security purposes," Alice explained with a chuckle. She called it the Black Beauty, and all the earlier houses were provided with them—the sole means of cooking. The wonder grew how Army procurement got hold of so many of these museum pieces.

At Mici's tea party that afternoon, under a clump of pine trees near the house, she explained, in her picturesque speech, her victory over the Army, often interrupting her tale to fetch a cup for some passerby invited to join the party.

"I told the soldier in his big plow to leave me please the trees here so Paul could have shade but he said, 'I got orders to level off everything so we can plant it,' which made no sense as it was planted by wild nature and suits me better than dust. The soldier left, but was back next day and insisted he had more orders 'to finish this neck of the woods.' So I called all the ladies to the danger and we put chairs under the trees and sat on them. So what could he do? He shook his head and went away and has not come again."

The Army personnel who ran the Post had orders from Washington to go easy on their charges and to make things as pleasant as possible. When they were cornered on little features, they gave in. Fuss and feathers again for General Groves.

After dinner that first day on the Hill, we sat on the porch of Fuller Lodge, the Ranch School dining hall, and looked at the view in the deepening twilight. I. I. Rabi, from New York, once remarked, "I envy all of you this magnificent view. None of you should complain about living here." Whereupon Emilio Segré, who did live on the site and did complain, answered, "Think how we shall hate even the view after living up here." But after two years, I never tired of it, changing in the shadows and the seasons.

Later that evening of our first day on the Hill, we wandered over to the theater after the movies to see the square-dance group that Sally Flanders had mentioned. The theater, built by the Army, was a bare barn-like structure that, nevertheless, managed to serve a multitude of purposes. George Hillhouse, chief butcher at the Commissary, was calling the squares with music from records. I was feeling some effects of the 7,000-foot altitude, but after getting spun around the floor by the dark and handsome George, I felt delightfully light-headed. The Flanders family, with their two teen-age daughters, Ellen and Jane, took Bob and my boys for whirls. Then, before we dropped from fatigue, we took our leave.

We walked home, passing the water tower, clear and sharp in the moonlight. As we came down the road to T-124, we heard someone playing the piano loud and vigorously in our house. The sound followed us through the thin walls. And so, on these notes, our first day ended at Los Alamos. It had been an exciting day.

Downtown Los Alamos was a combination of log cabins and jerry-built Army construction, with no paved streets and no sidewalks. The Trading Post at left was on Central Avenue near the site of the present post office.

A mid-'40's view of Los Alamos from the water tower shows the Ranch School power house in the foreground, the nursery school to the left of it, and Bathtub Row in the middle ground. Beyond that are Tech Area buildings and the Big House at the far right.

2 An Unusual Community

Los Alamos was an unusual community, beginning with its remote location high on a mesa. It was closed tight, exclusive to those chosen few possessing the magic pass. The only visitors were VIPs from high places in Washington who were directly connected with the Manhattan Project.

It was unusual because it was a young community with an average age of around twenty-five years. There were almost no old people, so those of us in our early forties were the senior citizens. We had no invalids, no in-laws, no unemployed, no idle rich and no poor.

The architecture in Los Alamos was unusual too—a combination of log cabins and the jerry-built Army construction that sprang up everywhere, inside and outside the fence and in adjacent canyons. Of the log and adobe buildings remaining from the Ranch School, there were large log houses along what came to be called "Bathtub Row," so named because these houses had the only bathtubs on the Mesa. Three of these were divided into several apartments each; two others were given to the Oppenheimers and to Navy Comdr. William S. "Deak" Parsons and his family. Another large house, once a house for the Ranch School's chief mechanic, was remodeled for the Post commanding officer. Two of the smaller buildings behind Fuller Lodge were renovated for the British Mission and smaller cabins near the Commissary housed several Post families. Across the field from the Lodge was "the Big House," a large two-storied dormitory where senior bachelors lived. One of two small stone buildings, formerly power houses, was made into one cozy room for George Kistiakowsky. There was also the school Trading Post, our first Post Exchange.

The Army engineers proceeded, in the early spring of 1943, to erect barracks and the technical area. Barracks for the Army personnel and dormitories for the civilians were built, and their occupants ate in the Army Mess Hall near the Big House. Families of Army officers and scientists lived in duplex or four-family apartments allotted according to family size. Every Army building was a nondescript green, and we soon referred to our dwellings as greenhouses. There were no sidewalks, no garages, no paved roads in town.

We also had a trailer area at the edge of the Mesa near East Gate. Sanitary conditions were a disgrace. Many of our socially minded ladies tried to get improvements, but in our last hectic days when the trailer area grew alarmingly, the authorities were too pressed to take any steps.

This, then, was the town where the first atomic bomb was made—plain, utilitarian and quite ugly, but surrounded by some of the most spectacular scenery in America. We could gaze beyond the town, fenced in by steel wire, and watch the seasons come and go—the aspens turning gold in the fall against the dark evergreens; blizzards piling up snow in winter; the pale green of spring buds; and the dry desert wind whistling through the pines in summer. It was surely a touch of genius to establish our strange town on the mesa top, although many sensible people sensibly said that Los Alamos was a city that never should have been.

The town's strangest feature of all, to us, was the security. We were quite literally fenced in by a tall barbed-wire barricade surrounding the entire site and patrolled on the outside by armed military police. In our first weeks we heard shots at night but never knew why. Actually, we felt cozy and safe to be free from marauders and mountain bears.

In our second year, extra MPs were sent to guard the homes of the Oppenheimers and Parsons, making round-the-clock patrols around the houses. No one, not even the families themselves, could go in or out without a pass. This could become awkward, as Kitty Oppenheimer and Martha Parsons were soon to learn. They often left their homes, unobserved, to visit neighbors only to find themselves unable to get back in without their passes. Martha called over to me once to come and identify her. I did my best but with all our giggling, neither of us could convince the MP. Finally, he watched as Martha went through her door, into a closet and, fortunately, found her pass at once.

Some of the practical housewives cooked up a scheme to use the MPs as baby sitters. What could be safer than a man with a gun guarding the precious small fry? The children were sure to be impressed and behave accordingly. Martha Parsons never hired a baby sitter as long as the MPs remained at her house. And Kitty Oppenheimer once got special service when her guard came to the front door of the house she was visiting to tell her that Peter was crying. Soon, alas, the sergeant in charge put his foot down—no more baby-sitting for his crack MPs, a group picked especially for duty at the number-one government project.

The patrol outside the fence soon ceased, too, except for an occasional mounted patrol. There was little temptation to "conquer" the fence, and no one tried except dogs and children who dug holes underneath to get through. Rather, the fence became a symbol. We felt protected and very important and tended to act accordingly, griping at everything including our fenced-in conditions.

Although we could leave the Mesa at will with a pass, we did have to keep within the boundaries, roughly defined by the New Mexico towns of Albuquerque, Cuba, Las Vegas, and Lamy, unless we got special permission to stay overnight or go to Mesa Verde, Denver, Carlsbad Caverns, or El Paso. We could not talk to friends or strangers on trips, and it was common knowledge that we were being watched by the Army G-2 and the FBI. We were not allowed to send our children to camp or away to school. If they were already in school, they could not come home for vacations.

Our drivers' licenses had numbers instead of names and were not signed; all our occupations were listed as "engineer," and our addresses as P.O. Box 1663. With gas rationing in effect, most of the traffic between Lamy and Santa Fe and Taos, was ours. All in all, it looked more than mysterious to the state police when any of us happened to be caught for a traffic violation. One day on the Taos road, a caravan of Army cars carrying a group of Nobel Prize winners and deans of science, all traveling under false names, was flagged down. When the officer asked the names of the occupants, each refused, as politely as possible, to give it.

"Tell that to the judge," retorted the officer as he wrote out a summons, determined to teach the almighty Army a lesson.

"I'm sorry, officer," ventured one of the men, "we can't appear either."

Finally the Army driver soothed the irate officer with a promise to take the summons to his commanding officer who would look after it. It took the CO and the governor of New Mexico to come to an understanding.

In the fall of 1943, the *Daily Bulletin*, delivered by a soldier and thrust in the kitchen door, surprised us with the announcement that all mail, incoming and outgoing, would be censored. The news caused quite a stir and a number of questions about its fairness, necessity, and legality. We were always accusing Army management of being dramatic about such things. In our neighborhood Hans Staub, a Swiss physicist, voiced our doubts about the goings-ons. "Thees iss nonsense. We do not want to give secrets away. We want to beat the Huns. That's why we come up here at all."

As censorship began, we had to apply for cards to send to relatives stating that mail was being opened for security purposes and asking that they destroy the cards and not mention the censorship at all. We sent our mail unsealed, with the understanding that it would be read, sealed and sent on by the censor. If something inside did not meet with the censor's approval, it would be returned to the writer with slip enclosed indicating what rule had been broken. We each had a book of rules describing what not to say. We could not mention last names, give distances of places nearby, and the word "physicist" was forbidden. We were assured that the censors were faceless persons who lived off the site and knew none of us. But they were human and funny things happened.

Alice Smith returned a bill to an eastern store saying "enclosed please find check." It quickly came back with a note from the censor: "You forgot to enclose the check." My son Jack, a stamp collector, once got a letter from a stamp company asking the meaning of a note enclosed in Jack's letter and signed by the censor. I had the habit of decorating my epistles with pumpkin faces, with smiles or mouth down, but the censor would send my letter back each time one silly face appeared. I argued and persisted to no avail and finally had to give up my sketches to get my mail through.

Dick Feynman, a young theoretical physicist whose wife was

too ill to live on the Hill, sent her a letter every day full of codes to amuse her. It was only natural that Dick would attract the attention of the Security Office. Capt. Peer de Silva, in charge of security, argued back and forth, and Dick even offered to supply the captain with the means of cracking the codes for himself, but de Silva was not amused. Everyone else was.

Since Los Alamos—or more strictly speaking, P.O. Box 1663—was the only place in the United States where mail was censored, envelopes with the censor's seal became collectors' items.

We continued to live in a security-minded atmosphere for nearly three years. Actually, anyone who had wanted to could have given away secrets. But enough of us, while poking fun at security regulations, took our trusted positions seriously. Some of our neighborhood philosophers at Los Alamos foresaw implications in the secrecy formula. Hans Staub went around asking in emphatic tones of prophecy: "Are those big tough MPs, with their guns, here to keep us in or to keep the rest of the world out? There is an important distinction here and before I leave this place, I want to know the answer."

Security was strict. At the East Gate, guards checked the passes of everyone wanting to enter or leave the Hill.

Young scientists and engineers in the Army's Special Engineer Detachment march in formation.

3 The Army

The U.S. Army Corps of Engineers, Manhattan District, under the direction of Gen. Leslie M. Groves, ran the project in those early years. Most of us were civilians at Los Alamos. We found living on an Army post unique, and I'm sure the Army regarded all of us as equally strange. Ordinarily, Army officers run any post to suit themselves, setting the standards and following strict protocol. At Los Alamos things did not work that way at all. Of all civilians, probably the free-wheeling scientists, with their tradition of non-conformity, are the least likely to measure up to proper military standards.

Furthermore, there was a feeling that we were slumming it up there on our secluded Mesa, far from city and university life, and free from the need to keep up appearances. We truly believed in plain living and high thinking.

To counteract the Army regime, the civilians had a Town Council, appointed at first and later elected as the town grew. The Council was most unorthodox on an Army post, but Oppenheimer believed that a civilian governing body, though lacking in real authority, would serve a useful purpose. The Council met regularly, discussing problems of the day, and either took action itself or passed resolutions that were sent to proper Army offices.

On one occasion, according to the stories, Council members Sam Allison and Julian Mack offered to investigate a complaint from some of the residents that prostitutes were soliciting in the PX. After sitting in the PX one entire evening waving $20 bills, the two investigators reported back to the Council that the complaints appeared to be entirely unfounded.

From the very first week, I was conscious of living under the Army. A soldier came to the kitchen door while we were eating breakfast to deposit the Daily Bulletin put out by the Post. Mimeographed, stapled together and bearing the admonition, "The paper is for the site—keep it here," the Bulletin contained local orders and announcements and was the Army's sole means of notifying the townspeople of policies and regulations.

"Doc" Barnett, in his Army uniform, came to call one of the first mornings after we arrived when we were still slightly dizzy and nauseated from the altitude. Doc was young—just out of medical school—serious and very good looking with dense blue eyes. We were not really ill, but he made notes on the boys' medical records and came to call every day as he made the rounds of the neighborhood. He said he wanted to keep an eye on all his children to prevent real sickness.

In the house next to ours, little Mutsie Staub frequently cried at night. Doc could find nothing wrong with her so he suggested to her parents that she might be suffering from lack of security up here. "Hell, Doc, what's the matter with you?" her father replied. "I suffer from too damn much security up here and you say my daughter has not enough?

In my early days there were just three doctors: Jim Nolan a general practitioner and obstetrician who became so overworked with the delivery of babies into P.O. Box 1663 that he soon had to have assistance. Henry Barnett was the general doctor and the men had Louis Hemplemann, who remained a civilian.

The original hospital, a barracks-like shack, was run entirely by Pete, the nurse. She had red hair, a long face and a sardonic sense of humor. She was an especially good match for the prima donnas who refused to be considered sick even if they really were. Pete had a tough time keeping things going in her hospital. I used to see her, in white uniform, carrying trays of food over from the Lodge to her patients. She claimed she was a nurse of all work.

So many babies were born that the hospital had, at one time, nearly half its capacity used as a nursery. The whole town wanted to come and see the babies, especially when a little Oppenheimer was born. The sign "Oppenheimer" was placed over baby Toni's crib, and people filed by in the corridor for days to see the boss's baby girl.

General Groves complained about the rapid increase in population that immediately increased the housing problem and eventually would increase the school troubles. Rumor had it that the General ordered the commanding officer to do something about

By 1944 the hospital, a barracks-like shack, had expanded to accommodate more doctors and a growing clientele, particularly newborn babies.

the babies, but it was not clear what was done, if anything. Our population was young and vigorous and babies were free; what could the General expect?

In our first year we had two epidemic scares—first rabies in dogs, then polio.

It seemed as if everyone had brought a dog to Los Alamos, and with no security rules to bind them, they roamed over the Mesa at will. When one of them began attacking people and was found to have rabies, Doc Barnett had a few hectic days. He kept bitten people under observation, gave extra shots, issued orders in the *Bulletin* and did his best to prevent the panic that was spreading fast. We were so frightened that we obeyed all the rules without question. But when the dog owners got tired of keeping their pets inside or on a leash, they suggested putting the children on leashes and letting the dogs go free. Others began to talk of banning all dogs from the site in the interest of community health. The fat was in the fire, people threatened to leave, and it became a struggle of dogs versus children.

Then, almost on the heels of the first, came the second epidemic scare. A young teacher was stricken with polio and, since serious illness could not be cared for in our hospital, was taken to Bruns

Hospital in Santa Fe. She died a few days later, spreading the deepest gloom over our small and closely knit community. School was promptly closed. All children were ordered to remain indoors and not to visit each other. No one was allowed to go to Santa Fe. The Commissary was quiet and peaceful without dogs or children. Snow began to fall and the children pressed their noses to the glass panes, longing to go out and play. A stillness of death descended upon our Mesa. Mothers had to stop work and stay home with the children. Little groups of adults gathered on back porches to hear further developments, and Doc ordered mothers to report immediately any sign of fever or illness. The heart went out of everything in our community, and there were no parties of any kind for several weeks. Henry Barnett and Jim Nolan bolstered our shattered spirits, performing far beyond the call of duty to dispel the doom and gloom. We had faith that the doctors would pull us through, and they did.

We had only one store, the Commissary, run by the Army with the help of some civilian employees including the two butchers, George and Mack, and Bences Gonzales in charge of the vegetables. The Commissary was a large, pleasant affair and, at one point, included our "bank," a teller's window where checks could be cashed.

The Commissary, which closed frequently for inventory, was the project's only store.

Civilian butchers were responsible for meat rations in the Commissary's meat market.

Our worst quarrel with the Commissary was its frequent "closing for inventory." Although the closings were announced in the *Daily Bulletin* and on signs posted by the Commissary, they caused a wave of neighborhood borrowing along with many complaints to the Town Council. I always ran out of milk, and Mici Teller would be sure to come up for coffee. "Never in my life have I been acquainted with these inventories," she would say. "I think they are just having the excuse to all go to Santa Fe."

In the early days, newcomers were conducted on a sight-seeing tour around the Commissary shelves. Peg Bainbridge and Jean Bacher took me around on my second day on the site, before there had been any conversion from an Army store to a supermarket. The most spectacular shelves contained rows and rows of gallon jugs of imitation vanilla or lemon flavoring, two-gallon tins of tomatoes, peas or corn, large glass containers of Jell-O powder in all their delicious colors. "You're in the Army now, dear," sang Peg and Jean. There were also many items long since vanished from the shelves at home—chocolate, nuts, stuffed olives, tomato juice.

One of the crosses we had to bear the entire time was the milk situation. There was no delivery to houses, and delivery to the Commissary was uncertain and in quantities too small to go around.

If an alert housewife saw the trucks arrive, she would shout the news to her neighborhood and everybody would rush to get some before it gave out. Army procurement added more and more dairies to our supply, but our consumption increased faster. Mr. Gonzales, who had worked for the Ranch School, was in charge of the big old-fashioned refrigerator and tried to ration the milk. He put very carefully lettered signs on the ice box—"one quart to each person, please"—but everyone claimed to be buying for others as well as themselves. The civilians checking out groceries lost control over rationing discipline, too, but when they were replaced by Wacs, we were put in our places quite mercilessly.

Vegetables in those early days were laid out on a sloping counter also lovingly presided over by Mr. Gonzales, who was so gracious and polite that he had difficulty rationing anything in short supply, such as lettuce. He sprinkled his wares by hand and did his conscientious best to freshen up the very tired vegetables.

Army officers, usually with considerable experience in chain stores and hotels, ran the Commissary, bought the stock and set the policies. When we tried to institute reforms, we ran into the stone wall of Army protocol, so we turned to the Town Council to spotlight the vegetable problem. Our own investigations soon revealed that the vegetables made a long and arduous journey to Mr. Gonzales' counter and had a right to be tired.

Although lovely produce was grown in the valley ranches only a few miles from our town, our vegetables were grown in East Texas, passed through the Army distribution center at El Paso, sent by train to Bruns Hospital in Santa Fe and transferred to trucks for the ride to the Commissary, taking at least three or four days in all. When one of the majors (we called them all majors since we could not always diagnose rank correctly and felt safer promoting rather than demoting them) appeared before the Town Council to explain the Army procurement system, we were not impressed. A young housewife in jeans and pigtails stood up to say all she was interested in knowing about Army procurement was why local vegetables could not be purchased. After much prodding, the real reason came out. There was no ready cash. The citizens then unanimously passed a resolution requesting the commanding officer to raise cash and buy

The Post Exchange was a lively gathering place for soldiers and civilians.

local produce. The major predicted failure, but the cash came from someplace, and we soon had lovely local vegetables, teeming with vitamins. No one was happier than Mr. Gonzales. The major asked for a transfer off the Mesa.

The Army used the Ranch School's Trading Post for the first PX, adding drug store supplies, GI-type gifts and souvenirs, cigarettes, GI towels and T-shirts, and then a strange and intriguing line of luxury items. Jean and I bought one of the first gallon jars of brandied dates for $5. The expensive contents were so yummy that everyone hastened to lay in a supply, and they quickly disappeared, never to be replaced.

Although we shed tears and put on pressure to retain it, the attractive log Trading Post was soon torn down and replaced by a larger, more efficient Army PX with a soda fountain, juke box, lots of tables and a large dance floor in one open space. It was run mainly for the soldiers, but it was the only drug store and sole source of such amenities as comic books, newspapers (hours or days late), ice cream cones and Cokes. It was a lively place. In the late afternoon it was customary to see tables of sedate, colorful Indians sipping Cokes as they waited for Army busses to take them back to their pueblos, Anglo families having sodas and reading the just-arrived *Denver Post*, Hill teenagers reading comic books and chasing each other, soldiers with their girls feeding the juke box and drinking beer. Sometimes the uproar was deafening and the air filled with smoke, but the eyes of the quiet Indians sparkled with enjoyment at everything. In the evenings, the noise and scuffling increased and sometimes real fights took place. The school tried to have the PX declared off limits to teenagers after 8:30 but the Army refused.

General Groves visited frequently but did not live on the site and so, like an absentee landlord, mysterious and unseen, he got the blame for everything that went wrong. Jane (Mrs. Robert) Wilson complained to him that cooking at high altitude on her Black Beauty was impossible, and invited him to her duplex and cook dinner to prove it. Maybe the shipment of electric hot plates that was sent up for distribution soon after was the result of Jane's dinner party.

We had small benefits, courtesy of the Army. Soldiers cut and stacked wood outside our houses for our fireplaces and Black Beauties. Soldiers came with trucks and work gangs to collect garbage and trash and to fix plumbing and anything else. At Christmas, they went into the mountains and cut trees of every size for us to choose. Heating was taken care of by the Army, which seemed like easy living to those used to stoking their own furnaces. But our furnaces were very special.

The first stoking of furnaces came to be a sort of fall ritual on the Hill. Cold came early at our altitude and by the last of September a frosty chill swept down from the Jemez Mountains, turning the aspens golden. Indians were taking in their strings of chile peppers and corn and gathering piñon nuts for winter, and we went down to the valley for apples from the orchards.

At about this time, a notice appeared in the *Bulletin*: "In the near future, the furnaces will be put into operation. At that time, it is expected that there will be a small amount of dust blown into apartments. Inasmuch as there is no other way of removing dust from the ducts, your indulgence is requested."

We discovered, our first year, that this was a studied understatement. So the second year, remembering the clouds of soot emitted from the opening near the ceiling, we placed cheesecloth over the ducts to catch the worst of it. Although the blasts of sudden heat were likely to blow off the cloth, the soot content was reduced, but never to zero. Our furnaces would never have passed any city inspection, but then, we had none.

Each day before dawn during the furnace season, the crew of stokers arrived. They were an unworried lot who sang and beat rhythms on drums or cans and drank Cokes in the warn furnace room. We heard it all through the open ducts in the wee hours of the morning before anyone was fully awake. When they finally left, we would fall asleep again, only to be aroused by a sound like a tremendous waterfall, followed by the rush of hot air mixed with cinders. In the dining room at breakfast, the thermometer would register 90 degrees or, quite often, 50 degrees or below. Changing the thermostat had no effect whatever, much to the bewilderment of my mechanically minded family.

The Army admonished us to leave the furnaces strictly alone. In emergencies, the approved procedure was to notify the major and lodge a complaint. The major would then relay the complaint in English to the Spanish-speaking stoker gang who would, presumably, take care of the problem on the next tour of the furnaces. But our emergencies did not always lend themselves to the system.

In our house in an emergency—by common consent, when the inside walls sizzled when touched by a wet finger—a complaint would be duly lodged with the major. Then, while the chain of command began, some husband in our house—usually mine or Cyril Smith—would boldly march down, with fire in his eye, to the forbidden but unlocked furnace room. As everyone watched from the windows, he would seize a shovel, remove a mound of red-hot coals and dump them on the side of the road. This at once brought showers of congratulations for the brave men and reduced the heat so much that we were glad to welcome the stokers on their next visit.

Like the Black Beauties in our kitchens, the furnaces were museum pieces with their function further complicated by the uncertain ability of the stokers and the inferior quality of the coal. The black stuff came from Madrid, near Santa Fe, and was too poor to be used in any other part of the war effort. That is why we had so much of it.

The huge pile of coal for the entire project lay between our greenhouse and the next one where the Julian Macks, Jim Nolans,

Dana Mitchells and Sam Allisons lived. Trucks came and went at all hours of the day and night, hauling coal to all parts of the Mesa. Coal dust was one of the neighborhood ingredients, tracked inside by children and their pets.

Children loved the hunks of coal and the bins of cinders and coal dust so readily available. I once saw two toddlers—Peter Bretscher, whose father was with the British Mission, and Paul Teller—playing on our road, covered with black dust and sucking coals. Mici rushed out in horror, asking the onlookers, "Where shall I grab him to carry him in?" Both babies were put to soak in the deep laundry sinks.

In addition to the regular Corps of Engineers who ran the Post, a Special Engineer Detachment was sent up to work in the Tech Area. Although the Army had failed to get the senior scientists in uniform as it wanted to, it did succeed in enlisting the very young men who were students in engineering and physics—some of them with PhDs.

These SED boys were quite different from the regular Post soldiers. They looked, in spite of the uniforms, like budding professors instead of combat troops. Shortly after they came up to the Hill, some high brass from Washington came for a formal military review in the baseball field in front of the Big House. All of us came with our children to see the show. The MPs, the Post soldiers, the Wacs, and even the doctors made a fine showing as they marched across the field, but the newly arrived SED boys were terrible. They couldn't keep in step. Their lines were crooked. They didn't stand properly. They waved at friends and grinned. The situation was not helped by the fact that they received the loudest applause from the bleachers. The visiting brass let it be known that they were displeased, and one general even called them a disgrace to the Army.

But the SED boys worked long hours in the Tech Area. Although they often worked late into the night to meet a deadline, they were expected to arise at dawn for inspection and drill by tough sergeants from the regulars. Once, when a sergeant became irritated by his yawning, half-hearted crew and shouted, "You guys think I like this job, you got another think coming," one of the SED boys offered to lead the drill in his place. He shouted orders in imitation of the sergeant's voice: "Thumbs up. Thumbs down. Thumbs wiggle-waggle." Even the sergeant broke down and dismissed them. My husband and others who used the SED boys finally got their discipline relaxed, the drill stopped and bed inspection let go so they could sleep in the mornings.

We became accustomed to administrators and doctors in uniform, Wacs selling sodas and checking groceries, selling postage stamps and cashing checks, and military police with guns guarding fences and gates and keeping our comings and goings under their watchful eyes. Perhaps it gave us a sense of being part of the war effort. It certainly helped Santa Fe people believe we really were a war project. It was said they had their doubts.

The Tech Area, where the main work of the project was done, resembled a small factory ... but soon grew in several directions.

4 The Tech Area

The Technical Area—called Tech Area, T Area or simply T— where the main work of the project was done, resembled a small factory—a two-story clapboard building painted, of course, green. The windows were large and pleasant, like those in our houses, although innocent of any washing since the original putty was smeared on. Originally the one building, designed as a laboratory only, was built along West Road. But we soon grew in all directions, adding wings wherever possible.

The Tech Area had its own fence around it, and a special badge was required to enter the gate guarded by MPs. The badges came in assorted colors indicating the areas to which the bearer had access. White was the highest form, also admitting the wearer to the testing area in the canyons. Mine was orange; though one of the lower forms, it allowed me to roam at will inside T.

I worked for some months as a computer (as we computing machine operators were called then) in the theoretical wing at T. The theoretical section was a quiet place, the peace broken only by some young man, presumably with a bright idea, giving a lecture while walking up and down the corridor and in and out of rooms. In normal times, these men would have been giving lectures in universities to admiring students. Cooped up in a factory atmosphere where the whistle blew at 7:00 and 7:30 summoning them to the grind, they gave lectures to each other. I once saw Enrico Fermi hiking down the hall talking in lecture form. Behind him followed a crowd of men, straining to keep up with his stride and listen at the same time. I sometimes saw Oppenheimer, too, being followed, but more closely since his softer voice didn't carry as far as Enrico's. Someone once remarked as Oppie passed his door, "There goes the mother hen and all the little chickens." Sometimes several of them would gather in one room, putting figures on the blackboard, talking, always talking as they wrote. Excited voices, in all kinds of accents, carried far and wide through the open doors.

The physicists were divided, roughly speaking, into two varieties—the theoretical and experimental. The distinction often made among themselves was that the former know what's the matter with the door bell while the latter know how to fix it. (Whether they do fix it, of course, is another matter.)

Everyone wore casual clothes—jeans or old unpressed pants, open shirts and no ties. I don't recall seeing a shined pair of shoes during working hours. They all seemed to be enjoying themselves, as scientists always do when they ponder their problems together. No one has to drive them; they drive themselves when they have an intriguing problem—and so it was at Los Alamos. Even an outsider like me, with no idea what the problem was, could feel the inner urge for scientific solution.

I suppose I heard a lot of talk that even now is stamped "top secret," and I used to ask facetious questions when the talk seemed to get bigger than usual. I once asked Emilio Segré what on earth we were hatching up there. To put me in my place, he answered seriously: "Now, Bernice, you just listen to me. What we do here, if we do it, will make a revolution, like electricity did." I knew we were engaged in an important aspect of the war effort, but as for Emilio's revolution, I continued to discount it. Later he was proved right in many ways.

Each night, after everyone had gone home, MPs came into T to check on security violations. If they found any, they would simply write an appeal in the *Bulletin* next day for more vigilance, but once in a while they would crack down. One night after midnight, Hans Bethe was selected as their victim. He had left something out of the safe so two MPs came to his house, woke him up and insisted he return to T and put the stuff away himself to teach him a lesson. Everyone was more careful from then on.

The usual percentage for part-time work was three-eighths never one-half or three-quarters. Why it was three-eighths remained one of our favorite top secrets. When a notice appeared in the *Bulletin* asking for applicants for this three-eighths-time computer work, several of us applied. Although none of us was trained in science or math, they needed help quickly, and we were accepted.

We were trained as computers by Joe Hirschfelder, a chemistry professor and ballistics expert. Joe was bald, of uncertain age, wore thick glasses, and tacked up *Esquire* calendars in his office "for decoration and cheerfulness." His secretary was a Santa Fe girl in tailored clothes and high heels, her hair in perfect order. She told us, eyeing our sweatshirts, jeans and sandals, that before coming to the site she worked for a bank in Santa Fe "where everything was of the best, Mrs. Brode. You could not run a bank like this." She was not used to the untidy professors and could never bring any order out of Joe's desk. I feared she would not last long in our makeshift world, and I was right. She left one morning, presumably for a more orderly world with filing systems, venetian blinds and wall-to-wall carpets.

Joe, a bachelor at that time, insisted that his mother be allowed to come up and keep house for him. He told Vera at the Housing Office that his mother was advanced in years and should have a lower apartment, usually reserved for families with young children, so she would not have to climb stairs. On the day she arrived, she took a lengthy hike up a steep trail, "to see the splendid view, don't you know."

Mrs. Hirschfelder, or "Ma," as we affectionately called her, was short and stout with a ruddy complexion. She wore black dresses, high black shoes and a large black hat trimmed with pink roses. She walked everywhere, carrying a black umbrella in bad weather. She enthusiastically supported all activities and thought everything and everybody most amusing. She wouldn't have missed living on the Mesa for anything.

After three months of computer training, we were moved to the theoretical wing of T to work under mathematician Moll Flanders. After hours, Professor Flanders and his family contributed greatly to our musical life. All the family sang and played instruments, and Moll himself conducted our chorus and orchestra. He wore an unusual but becoming full beard, and when we asked why, he replied in his New England accent, "If you had three women in the family and only one bathroom, would you not do likewise?"

Moll put all of us in one room with machines around the edges and our desks pushed together in the center. This was a mistake, for we all sat facing each other, always tempted to discuss "Mesa business" in which we were all more knowledgeable than in the work at hand. Our immediate overseer was Mary Frankel, who set up the problems for us to run through the machines. The resulting figures were taken to the graph room, in the charge of Bob Davis, and were put on his graphs. The idea was to make curves, and all the scientists took the greatest interest in the progress of the curves. If our figures put a jog in one of the curves, the figures were wrong—not vice versa.

Mary had a small office near Moll's where she made out our problem sheets and put them in a basket marked "Free—take one." She was a young blonde with a doctorate who took her job very seriously and encouraged us to study math at night. She was fussy about decimal points and regarded our mistakes as appalling, which they probably were. "Mrs. B.," she would say to me, "There is a great future in this computing business if you could possibly learn decimals." Mary was a good twenty years my junior so I reminded her that "this is my future." I once asked her why we worked three-eighths time and she replied, "Mrs. B., if I could answer questions like that one, I would be in charge of this whole outfit."

Every room in T had a loudspeaker over which came diverting messages.

"Attention please. Will the person who took the Sears Roebuck catalog from Harold Agnew's room please return it immediately. Repeat—immediately."

"Attention please. Will the owner of the lady's blue bicycle with the outsized basket please remove it. The bulldozer is coming and the bicycle is in danger." I dashed out, for it sounded like mine. It was.

More frequently it was a call for the head janitor. "J. J. Gutierrez, J. J. Gutierrez, please. A major crisis is brewing. J. J. Gutierrez, J. J. Gutierrez, please." It was well understood in inner circles that the three top people running the project were General Leslie Groves, J. Robert Oppenheimer and J. J. Gutierrez.

The wing of the Technical Area where my husband and most experimental physicists worked was at the other end of the original T building. It was here that top-secret "know how" problems were solved. This was the noisy part of the Technical Area with the hum of machinery sometimes shaking the floor. The large labs adjoining the offices were full of enormous gadgets, labeled with crude warning signs like "Caution—live wires," " Test well before using," "Watch light," "Keep out," "Don't handle," or "Wear lead." I was most careful where I stepped and never tried to sit. All chairs were likely to be holding sharp tools or bits and pieces and parts. Long rolls of paper were emitted from a machine, and the men tending all the machines had that characteristic rapt expression. The din was terrible, and people had to shout to be heard.

When the Wacs arrived, well trained as computers, wives were permitted to quit, and only a few of the wives—those without children—stayed on. I was allowed to keep my orange badge, however, so I could get into T to run errands or pick up our mail. We had no mail delivery to our homes, and when my husband was off the Mesa, as he frequently was, I would get no mail. There was also a certain prestige involved in having a badge. Many persons in our town lived there all through the war years without a peek inside the Tech Area.

Salaries were paid according to the last job held, resulting in many inequities. But this was accepted as a sacrifice of the war, for there was no time to work out another salary scale for everyone. Young men from lucrative jobs in industry and hired for routine work on the project were often paid handsomely while senior professors from universities, who bore much of the burden of the project, received much less. Young men without PhDs often contributed important ideas but got stipends no more than meager fellowship grants. To compensate, we were charged rents according to salary, not rank.

We were all cut down to size at Los Alamos, and it was sometimes a sobering experience. Even Oppie abandoned his former pattern of living. I remember the days when he would not accept a class before 11:00 in the morning so he could feel free to stay up late for parties, music, or ideas. But at Los Alamos, when the whistle blew at 7:30, Oppie would be on his way to T, and hardly anyone would beat him to it. When Sam Allison came to the site from Chicago, he shared Oppie's office for some time. Sam said his one ambition was to be sitting at his desk when Oppie opened the door.

Apartment house T-124 was typical of all those built later. The families within were typical, too, representing a cross section of nationalities and personalities to be found in Los Alamos.

5 Apartment House T-124

Our four-family apartment house, T-124, was one of the first of the Army-built houses and typical of all those that were built later. The four families who lived in it, too, were quite representative, forming a cross section of the nationalities and personalities to be found in Los Alamos. In the years our family lived in T-124 C, we put down whatever roots were possible. I became very much attached to our greenhouse and to other families and look back on these days with nostalgia.

Oppenheimer described the houses as "pleasant," particularly in our area where they were irregularly placed to follow the mesa terrain. Although I never checked it, rumor had it that each of them cost the Army more than $65,000 to erect even with the cheapest, flimsiest of building materials. Outside they were the usual green-painted wooden clapboards, and inside, the plaster board was covered with a dull, non-washable cream-colored paint. The walls got dirty very fast, but each year the Army sent in the usual 10-man crew to redecorate. This was an ordeal, as the crew took over for several days and made a fine mess. Mary Mack, in the next house to ours, insisted a small square of the original ceiling be left as it was to show how the furnaces darkened the interiors. Some families got ambitious and bought real paint in chosen colors in Santa Fe and did their own walls, but no one in our house got around to it.

All the kitchens faced on the road, so that the fronts of the houses were really the backs. Callers came in via the back, or kitchen, doors from the steps that were just off the road. The front entrances—in our case, the mountain view side—led nowhere, and since we had no walks, the mud alone kept the front doors from being much used. There was no sun on the front porch of our house, so we only sat there when we wanted to escape the summer heat. The narrow back runway porches got full sun, and since they faced the road where life was going on, we sat on the steps for gossip and morning coffee.

The Brodes lived in one upper apartment and the Cyril Smiths in the other. Below the Smiths were the Edward Tellers, and below us were the Felix Blochs until Felix left for another project. Later their apartment was taken by the Egon Bretschers of the British Mission. Although the apartments were identical—or mirrored identical— each took on the color of the inhabitants. Robert Oppenheimer once told me, "Everyone in your house is quite mad. You should get on fine together." And so we did, although there were quarrels and we got in each other's hair, mainly because of our various children and our lack of privacy.

We became closer to the Smiths than to the others, partly because we shared the upper stairs and balcony and had a common storeroom. When I returned to Berkeley after the war years, one of the things I missed most was watching Alice go by my kitchen door and observing what mood she was in at the moment.

With her full-time job teaching social science at the Upper School (seventh to twelfth grades), Alice had a high priority for maid service, but the maids came after she had left or not at all. I went to work at T much later, so if the maid didn't show up, I would go into Alice's house and at least clear away the breakfast dishes. The men and children came home at noon for lunch, so it was a scramble for Alice to get back to school by one o'clock. I could put in my three eighths time at Tech on any basis I liked, which made my life much easier than Alice's. Since my two boys were benefiting from Alice's teaching, I always felt obligated to her but could do little in return.

Alice was a tall and willowy blond, very beautiful when she rested and dressed up to teach or for social occasions. Her standards were higher than mine—she could not wear casual clothes for teaching, and did not like them anyway. She could not let things go and relax. Alice always seemed restless, even when she curled up on my sofa with a cup of coffee saying she was too tired even to talk. If I chanced to say the wrong thing to her, those blue eyes would flare up in anger, and sometimes she would go out my kitchen door and bang it to relieve her feelings. The issue was so unimportant that one of us was sure to try and make it up immediately after. Living so close together, it was all too easy to touch raw spots in the ego. A friend of ours once said she believed Alice and I liked to have tiffs so we could make up and perhaps have a good cry. The very air around Los Alamos was emotionally charged, and our high-pitched morale, of which the General was so proud, took its toll.

The Smiths, unlike us, had brought along their books, so Cyril made shelves for them and we all used their library. I had a piano, not as elegant as the Tellers', but Alice loved to play it and sing. It was kept in better shape than it ever had been before, as Edward arranged for a tuner to come up from Santa Fe every month, and we all had to get our pianos tuned to provide the man with a day's work. I told Edward he ought to learn to tune his own piano, like our neighbors, the Jorgensons did. It took them all year, and by the time they were finished with the last key, it was time to begin all over again.

Alice's and my kitchen equipment was quite interchangeable, especially hot plates and electric ovens. For any sizable dinner, one needed at least two ovens. Sometimes we cooked together, even if we ate the meals separately. Our houses were not wired for anything drawing more juice than appliances, and even so we could not plug in all the appliances we had collected. Because there was a chronic shortage of electricity, we were admonished through the *Daily Bulletin* to save on electricity. Often in the middle of dinner preparations, with every housewife plugging in for cooking, the current would be turned off without warning. When this happened in winter, we scurried around for candles and put more logs in the fireplace to finish cooking there. The Black Beauties took too long to get going for emergencies, so most of them remained as picturesque tables for all appliances.

Cyril Smith was British-born and not as outgoing as his wife. He was very tall and distinguished looking. Although he appeared severe, he could unbend at parties and be a lot of fun with his sharp wit. He spoke with a slight hesitation of speech when angry, and he could get quite angry when he stumbled over some sharp radio or electric "part" my son Bill had left along our mutual stairs and balcony. In turn, my husband, also tall, distinguished looking and quite severe when angry, would sound off at something Stevie Smith had done, but that was life at T-124 C and D.

The Smiths kept to a regular and rigid schedule, so it was no wonder that they regarded the irregular hours kept by the Tellers, who lived beneath them, as a hardship. The floors and walls were so thin that every sound came through. Neither Edward nor Mici nor the baby Paul, called Piggily, even tried to keep to a routine. It was not in their Hungarian temperaments, and apparently Edward's part in the work did not require his getting over to T at any set time. Edward was always being kidded about his lack of hours at T, but he took the jests lightly. He and Mici were both individualists, which made them delightful company at parties. When Alice complained that they were kept awake at night, Mici said tearfully that it wasn't her fault that Edward got all his bright ideas at night and wanted to discuss them with her. She wanted to sleep, too.

It was usually near noon when Edward emerged, still deep in thought, and slowly walked up the road to T. He never seemed to have a sense of urgency, which I found restful. Mici, on the other hand, was always hurrying to make sudden plans that just had to be carried out then and there, like her tea party on my first day in Los Alamos. Her enthusiasm for going places and doing things was enormous, so everybody included her in arrangements for trips. She was excellent company and generous to a fault.

She could always leave Edward to shift for himself, but Paul had to be provided for. Her familiar question posed to the neighborhood was, "Would anyone care to have Paul?" My boys always said, under their breath, "The answer is NO." Little Piggily was a delightful child with his big brown eyes and his head covered with dark ringlets, but he was a handful. He walked early and succeeded in getting around and out of any fenced-in situation contrived for his welfare. Unlike Cyril and Bob, Edward was not too useful in making fences and other contraptions needed by our children from time to time. Mici complained that Edward promised but never got around to anything, so she tried to hire the work done. Piggily wandered away from his rigged-up barricades so often that her anguished cry of "Paul is lost" soon made my boys very hard-boiled about getting on their bicycles to hunt for him. Jack would say, "Aw, Mom, relax. He'll get home somehow." This was quite true. Someone always found him and brought him in. Edward said, "I'm glad my son won't be fenced in, otherwise I should worry about him."

Sometimes Mici's arrangements for Paul got so complicated that even the mathematician John von Neumann had trouble with them. Johnny didn't live on the site but was a frequent visitor and good friend of the Tellers. One day during one of his visits, he joined a carload of us going to Santa Fe, leaving Edward in charge of Paul for the evening. Mici decided she wanted to stay overnight in Santa Fe to get a real bath and a good sleep, returning home by the Army bus the next day. So before we left Santa Fe, she made out a schedule for Paul and entrusted it to Johnny to relay to Edward. On our way home, Johnny rehearsed his instructions. Edward was to put Paul to bed and should be reminded to undress the baby first and put him into pajamas. Next morning, Edward would get Paul up (or "vice versa," predicted Johnny), feed him and wait for the half-day maid to come at 8:30, when Edward would be free. But first he was to tell the half-day maid to get Paul ready for nursery school. Then Paul was to be taken over to Honi Bretscher who would take him to nursery school along with her son Peter. Since Mici, on the Army bus, would

Edward Teller, with Paul on his shoulders, talks science with David Inglis and Julian Schwinger.

not arrive on the Hill until 2 P.M., there was still Paul's lunch and nap unaccounted for. Johnny promised to confer with Edward about this discrepancy, with the probable result that the two men would get to discussing physics and forget all about Paul.

The Teller living room was dominated by Edward's Steinway grand piano. His playing at all hours was another house problem, but Edward was reasonable and desisted from his habit of playing very early on Sunday morning, the only day the Smiths could sleep late. He could play quite well but admitted he played mostly to relieve his feelings, rather than to make music. Poor Edward; we all got after him, for his banged feelings came up to our apartment, too. Because the climate was so dry, he kept a basin of water under the piano. No matter what defenses were set up, Paul got at it at least once a day and dumped it.

One nice thing about Mici was her lofty disregard of a mess in her house. I always felt welcome at any time, no matter what the floor situation turned out to be. Once I went into the Tellers' kitchen to see if they were up yet and found Paul getting his own breakfast on the floor. He had taken a bottle of milk from the refrigerator, leaving the door open, and poured about half a quart into a large mixing bowl that he must have pulled onto the floor from a low cupboard. Into this bowl he had dumped sugar from a large bag, a good deal of sugar missing its target. As I came upon him, he was filling the dish with one whole box of corn flakes and began at once to eat the mixture with a tablespoon as he squatted on the floor. He must have been chilly, since he was not exactly clothed. A box of soap flakes had somehow been overturned in the process and been liberally scattered around as Paul went about his serious business. It was slippery and crunchy anywhere I stepped. I was about to bow out when Mici came in and exclaimed, "Gracious, what is Paul doing?" It was quite obvious, and since he was happy, we went into the living room to have a smoke. The Indian maid would clean up next time she came.

On the other side of the house, we also had adjustments to make. Complaints against the Brodes included the fact that two big boys were heavy-footed and noisy, rode their bicycles too fast down the road, endangering the many little kids always playing in the road or near it. My boys insisted they had good brakes and perfect control and could stop instantly. In turn, they complained that the kids overturned the bicycles propped against the side of the house. So my husband offered to construct a bicycle rack with enough space for the Smith bicycles. Since the families in the lower apartments owned no bicycles, both objected to giving play space to the rack. Mici and Bob had a to-do about the possibility of building it around in front, which would mean we would get very muddy getting into the house. Bob was firm and built the rack near the house coal bin, between the two apartments in back, and the little ones eventually learned to leave our bicycles alone. The worst hazard was Bill's room, where he carried on chemistry and electronics projects.

The Felix Blochs, Swiss-born and parents of two-year-old twin boys, lived below us when we arrived. I offered to baby-sit for the twins, an easy job since we could hear them from upstairs through the thin ceiling. One night, while we were having a dinner party, Bill came in from his room, which was just over the twins, and reported a great commotion was going on below. I went down with Jean Bacher, one of our guests, to find that the twins definitely were not sleeping nicely. Each baby had a crib with a cover latched down, but the aggressive twin had got out anyway, unlatched his brother's crib, and was throwing everything he could find on top of the half-asleep twin. Jean and I cleared out dirty and wet clothes, clean starched shirts, and even a pair of Felix's shoes, and quickly put the place and the twins to rights.

The Blochs once put a notice in the *Daily Bulletin* that a player piano could be had for the taking. The twins operated this piano tirelessly, and it drowned out Edward's playing. No one took up the offer, so when the Blochs moved out and the Army refused to move the piano, they deposited it outside, just off the road. One moonlit evening, Edward came by and gave a concert that could be heard all over the Mesa. When a crowd gathered around, Cyril Smith suggested passing a hat to take up a collection to have the piano moved. Nevertheless, it remained there for weeks in rain and shine. Finally my husband gave the go-ahead to my eager boys, who began dismantling the insides of the piano, assembling the parts for future use in their many projects. It kept them busy for weeks.

The Bretschers, who came to live below our apartment after the Blochs left, were also Swiss-born, but were British subjects. They had three small children: baby Peter; Mark, age 4; and Scilla, age 8. The Army did its GI best to furnish the house nicely, but even so it looked sparse and a little dreary. Alice, Mici and I tried to brighten it up for their arrival with flowers, a few utensils, and a loaf of home- made bread placed on the sink. We hesitated to rush matters, as the new family was not only unknown but foreign as well, so we called on them only after they seemed well settled in their house. We thought we were being most reserved, but the Bretschers told us later they were quite overcome by such an effusive—and unexpected—welcome.

The senior Bretschers were reserved and appeared more British than Swiss. Honi was the intellectual type, retiring and thoughtful by nature, but forced to activity in caring for her family. She was not allowed to take a job on her visa, but was allotted some maid service anyway, a privilege given to the British families and to Martha Parsons and Kitty Oppenheimer. Honi wore heavy tweed skirts and turtleneck sweaters all the time and, of course, suffered from furnace heat. Since the heat couldn't be regulated by thermostat, Honi finally was forced to get cotton blouses, and toward the end of their stay, she even wore jeans. I always felt that she seemed uneasy with the "hectivity" in our house and the breezy comings and goings of Alice, Mici and me.

Egon Bretscher, or Gon, as he was sometimes called, was tall and handsome but forbidding-looking. A true Swiss, he loved our mountains at once. He went for long walks by himself, assuming no one could possibly keep up with him. He was more of a disciplinarian than the other fathers, and all the little Bretschers moved fast when Papa spoke, while the neighborhood children gaped in amazement. I never felt that his wife approved of his severity, but she backed him up. I was distressed, because so often at breakfast we heard one little Bretscher or another go into a tail-spin and have a crying jag. My Jack would raise his eyes from his cereal, "Papa spank again." By the time they left for school, all smiles, Scilla and Mark would cling to Papa's hand as they went up the road. I began to suspect that Gon was a softy inside and used his bark to cover up. He often played on Edward's piano with a gentle touch, much more musical than Edward's, although his repertoire was not as large. The Staubs in the next house also were Swiss, although very Americanized, and they visited the Bretschers often.

Little Scilla and Mark Bretscher spoke beautiful King's English when they came on the Hill and all the children listened in wonderment. "Why do you talk so funny?" Annie Smith asked. Not only their speech but their clothes were different. They wore woolen socks and shined leather shoes, tailored blouses and jumpers or short pants, and tweed overcoats. So we watched with interest the changeover to T-shirts and short socks, jeans and gingham dresses, and realized that someday the process would have to be reversed in England.

There is no question about it, we lived too close together and our walls were too thin. All of our men were under strain. The job was hard, and they were working against a deadline to construct the weapon before the Germans did. None of the men was used to working under a large administrative setup. The senior men, especially, had their own ideas and methods and were used to getting on with their own work in their own time. If they hadn't felt the call of patriotic duty, they wouldn't have come to Los Alamos in the first place, so most of them made a great effort to adjust, and since they were reasonable men of good will, the results were tensions, usually at home.

But in spite of everything, or possibly because of everything, our house was very congenial, and we had some wonderful times together. The same could be said for many other four-family greenhouses as well. They all had stresses and strains, with conflicting personalities, but many houses, like ours, gave four family progressive parties, treating the entire house as one for the occasion.

Alice and I, as the only American wives in our house, initiated a Thanksgiving dinner. We invited a good share of the foreign-born colony on the Hill, as well as the four families in the house, a total number that warranted three turkeys roasted in three electric ovens. One afternoon when Laura Fermi came to help me stuff my turkey, we sat by my table meticulously chopping ingredients just as she said was done in her native Italy. Still dazed by nostalgia for her country, Laura found little comfort in our hectic routine on the Hill. Would all this push and rush pay off? she wondered. In America she had been pressed too much into affairs and values she questioned, so we argued all afternoon on such topics while we cut onions, suet, bread, and celery. Newly arrived on the Hill, the Fermis lived on the West Road in one of the second batch of greenhouses. The West Road was the main line of traffic from the gates to the Commissary and the Technical Area. She said her area was full of construction and noise, and our end a bit quieter. However, as we talked, I looked down and counted twenty-two children within sight of our table.

The guests for Thanksgiving dinner assembled at Mici's apartment for cocktails and hors d'oeuvres, beautifully arranged on platters. Afterward we left the mess for her next half-day to clean up, and everyone filed upstairs to Alice's apartment for the main course.

Bob and Cyril had set up plank tables running continuously from the fireplace to the other end of the room, making a quarter turn to the windows of the dining nook. Those sitting on the far side of the table had to duck under to reach their places. We brought on all three turkeys, looking delicious but presenting a carving problem since none of the foreign men felt trained to carve a bird. Bob, the only American-born man present, went to work on the first turkey, Cyril finally decided to take over the second bird, and my boys tried the third one. They had never done it before but had watched their father many times. Gon Bretscher, used to British rations, said he hadn't seen a turkey in years and didn't care how it was carved up. I can't imagine how we got all the vegetables, gravy, and fixings cooked and served, but we did, for Alice and I had insisted on all the traditions of the feast.

The next move was for salad in the Bretschers' apartment, leaving the Smith's apartment practically uninhabitable. We helped ourselves to salad from the sink board and sat on the floor to eat since all the chairs and tables in the house were at Alice's. Everyone was so full by this time that they lingered and talked before going upstairs to our apartment for pie and coffee. I had made several mince and pumpkin pies the day before and one apple for Edward since he insisted he didn't like the other kinds. It was our only deviation from American Thanksgiving tradition.

We all had dinner guests frequently, quite often at the last minute when new young men or VIPs came to the Hill. The Lodge could not accommodate all who wanted to eat there, and the Mess Hall was out of the question. The young bachelors who were forced to take meals there regularly told tales of standing in long lines in winter with ice cold trays that congealed the food as it was thrown on. Our hearts went out to them, so we invited them for home dinners as much as possible. They would be happy to come anytime and helped wash the dishes. Alice and I both agreed that we had never fed so many men so many meals in all our lives. Finally, in our last year, a cafeteria was opened, offering good food and a steak night once a week, but never advertised in advance for obvious reasons. It was a welcome addition, since by then we were tired of serving people meals with rationed meats, carrying all supplies down on bicycles, cooking at high altitude on hot plates with uncertain electricity.

It was the fresh vegetables from the garden of our friend Edith Warner, down by the river at Otowi Bridge, that made the biggest impression on Mess Hall habitués. Unlike the families, they had meat every day, even if it was cooked gray, as the boys said. But vegetables at the Mess Hall were out of those large cans from the Commissary. If I got a windfall from Miss Warner's garden, I dispatched my boys around in the dorms to invite young men and also any new school teachers. Single women were scarce at dances and dinners. It was a man's world on the Hill, and sometimes I had more than a dozen males to feed when I was the only woman. I didn't mind.

Strictly speaking, there was no such thing as a house guest at Los Alamos. VIPs, our only town visitors, were put up at the Lodge. Nevertheless, we had an overnight guest one time, an utter stranger to me. He was a mild-appearing man who made a spectacular entrance in the middle of the night, accompanied by two burly MPs. His visitor's pass was not at the gate as it should have been, and as he said he was coming to see my husband, the MPs brought him into our house. I was aroused by a loud knock at the back door and went to see, expecting Alice or Mici with some emergency about the children. The biggest MP asked if I could vouch for this man, but I had never seen him before in my life. I had to waken Bob, who, fortunately, was able to identify the stranger. The guards let him stay with us instead of taking him to the Lodge at that time of night.

The bewildered man had had a rough trip by air, and the reception at the gate unsettled him. We put him to bed on our living room couch, and in the morning I tiptoed past him hoping he could sleep, late, although the usual early morning noises at T-124 would awaken the dead. Just as he was waking up, probably wondering where he was, Mici, clad only in her bathrobe, burst in the front door to borrow some coffee. When she saw a strange person in bed, she stopped and put her hand over her mouth to suppress a scream. She dashed into the dining nook where we were having breakfast as quietly as possible, exclaiming, "There is a strange man in there. Did you know?' I explained in a whisper, gave her the coffee, and she went out very excited. The tale spread over the Mesa grapevine, gathering details as it went.

.

6 Maid Service

It was not required for our welfare at Los Alamos that our maid service be so picturesque; it was just one of those things that seemed to come naturally. It lent color to our lives, like the scenery around us.

Every working day the Army sent buses down to the pueblos where Indians lived and to the settlements where the Spanish Americans lived, and picked up the recruits to bring up to the Hill. They were deposited at the Maid Service Office, situated in one of the pleasant old buildings, a Ranch School garage beside the water tower. The garage had two rooms, one for the girls as a headquarters for the day, and the other for the Maid Service Office. On the walls of the latter hung a chart for the week, showing which girl was to go to which house or dorm for the morning and for the afternoon. That is why we referred to them as "half-days." They ate their lunches in the garage in bad weather or sat under trees around the Mesa on nice days. Sometimes they ate in the PX, but usually they saved a visit to the PX for the day's end while waiting for the buses.

The chart on the office represented the attempt to allot the maids fairly, and involved importance of the housewife's job, numbers and ages of children, and temporary illness. (We were all healthy or we should not have come up there to live.) The general idea of providing maids was not to make life leisurely but to enable the wives to take jobs on the site, and hence keep the population at a minimum. The simplicity of the chart on the wall was misleading. The human factor could play havoc with it.

First of all, there were the Saints' Days and Feast Days and the days preceding when the girls stayed at home to prepare for them. These days were not celebrated on our project, nor was it easy to find out from the girls in advance how many days they would be absent. A shortage of maids caused Vera Williams and her assistants the trouble of deciding all over again which housewives deserved help the most. Was Alice Smith's job teaching at the school more important than Kay Manley's job as secretary in the Tech Area? Could Alice's two children shift for themselves better than Kay's two little girls?

The difficulties in our priority system were often compounded by the girls themselves, who developed their preferences for certain families. Most of them disliked being switched around at the whim of the chart, and they often went where they pleased anyway. So many times those women who received no help marched up to the bureau and demanded to know why no half-day arrived. Mici always called the girls "helps" and never accepted the notion that she could not have as many helps as she was willing to pay for. The maids got $3 per day, $1.50 for 8:30 to 12:00, or 1:00 to 4:30. Sometimes we had a surplus for the day, whereupon Vera sent the girls around to houses usually willing to accept them on a moment's notice.

And so each morning, except Sundays, as we sat at breakfast, one of the sights on the road was groups of Indian women coming slowly past the water tower to our houses. They dressed in pueblo fashion—short, loose, colorful mantas tied with a woven belt, high white deerskin-wrapped boots or just plain stout walking shoes, gay shawls over the head and shoulders, and enough turquoise and silver jewelry to stock a trading post. All of them, young or old, had such serene dignity that they seemed more like guests than servants.

Very few had ever worked outside their own homes. Things like vacuum cleaners defeated them, but they understood linoleum floors and our Black Beauty stoves and made them shine. They talked little, although most of the Indians knew three languages—English, Spanish and their native Tewa. What they thought of our strange town or our houses—many of them with Indian rugs, pottery and paintings—we shall never know. They did not rush about as we did, but worked slowly. All in all, the maids were delightful and were of some help.

Pat, a very fat and good-natured Indian from San Ildefonso Pueblo, was assigned to Alice, and each morning she went by our kitchen door to the Smiths. Of uncertain age, she wore long black bangs to her eyes with the rest of her long hair in a knot in back. She took off her shawl and hung it on the back of the kitchen door, removed her jewelry and stacked it on Alice's sink board, then went about her work in her own way, heedless of instructions Alice left on the sink. Pat could read all right; it was just her easy-going nature and habits. Instead of getting out the vacuum cleaner, she took the Oriental rugs out on the back porch and shook them vigorously, right over the heads of babies playing below. Pat was very friendly and often brought Alice and me presents—a loaf of the round bread made in the beehive ovens, or a piece of her mother's pottery. So many of us made so much over her delicious bread that Pat brought up the entire batch one day and asked me, "You sell to ladies for me?" I was a little taken aback, but I said yes—but for 25 cents a loaf, not the 75 cents she slyly suggested. She once asked busy Alice to stuff a chicken to take down to the pueblo for a celebration. Good-hearted Alice did it, but remarked to me, "Who is working for whom?"

Appolonia from Santa Clara Pueblo was one of my regular maids—I didn't rate one every day like Alice—and she walked down the road with Pat. Appolonia was thin and quite old, with corkscrew curls lining her pointed face. She often brought me thin tortillas made from blue corn, or pottery candlesticks made like the high pueblo boots. When I learned the maids from these two pueblos were brought up an hour before work, I invited them to my house for coffee on cold mornings. Several times they came and sat silently beside my family, sipping coffee and seeming to enjoy themselves. When my men hurried off and I went into the kitchen, I would hear the Indians giggle, although I never found out why.

As new families came up to the Hill, the Army made an effort to increase the maid service, too, but, like everything else in our town, there was always a shortage of girls. We never had enough help. We would have loved to have the girls stay overnight to help with parties and dinners, but this was strictly forbidden. Some Spanish girls lived on the Hill, but worked full time at the Lodge, dorms, or at the PX and were not available to us.

Men came up in the Army buses, too, for work as janitors, stokers, and at general tasks. They were more taciturn than the women and not as gaily dressed. Most of them wore work clothes, but their hair was unusual—either a Dutch cut and a bandeau around the head, or two long braids tied at the ends with yarn. When we saw these same men at their ceremonial dances, in fancy costumes and beating drums, they were different persons to us.

The maids shopped at the Commissary for groceries to take back to the pueblos, then sat in the PX, which they loved, sipping Cokes or sodas until the Army drivers announced departure of the buses. The Army once issued orders in the Daily Bulletin that no one who did not live on the site could purchase in the Commissary, due to difficulties in getting enough supplies. I'm sure they did have troubles keeping up with our growing population, but we all protested vigorously against this ban on our maid service. There were no stores in the pueblos where supplies could be had, and since the women worked all day for us, they could not go to Española or Santa Fe to buy, nor did they cultivate their own lands much. So the Army took off the ban, and we were glad, although the maids often cut short their afternoon half-days to go shopping before the buses left.

I think the Indians, especially, loved their daily trips to this other world. The extra money was more than they had ever had, and new additions to houses, new furniture and even a few inside bathrooms attested to the influence upon them from Los Alamos. While we collected their crafts for our homes, they seemed to prefer Anglo tastes.

The school was exceedingly well built with picture windows looking out over a super view. It matched the early concept of a super school with super children of super parents, all adding up to super education.

7 The School

Our school at Los Alamos was the most exclusive in the country—and our worst problem. In the beginning, everyone was completely unrealistic about the school, and we all had to learn the hard way. The earliest organizers seemed to proceed on the assumption that the school would be the least of their troubles. With all those thoroughly educated people to be hired, why wouldn't it be a cinch to set up and run a fine school for their kids? I shared this smug optimism myself. Here was a chance of a lifetime to put our own ideas on education into practice. When 1 heard that we of the new community could run our own school, I had visions of my boys learning perfect French from Peg Bainbridge, who had taught at Radcliffe, of some of the country's finest chemists teaching my Bill the advanced work for which he was ready, and so on. Pick any subject and there would be some expert in that field ready and eager to teach our children.

To get off to a grand start, the Manhattan District hired a Midwest educator to make a survey. The survey was kept top secret for some time, but we got hold of a copy about the second year. It revealed the concept of this super school with super children of super parents, all adding up to super education. I imagine the educator planned to follow it up with a future study of the super results.

The survey laid down plans for a super building, too, and this we had. The fine modern structure was exceedingly well built to last one hundred years, whereas the Technical Area and our houses were jerry-built with no assurance that they would last out the war. We loved our beautiful school building, with its picture windows looking out over a super view, and we used it for meetings and parties as well as for classes. Rumor had it that the General was a bit less than pleased with the construction. According to the story, the original plans called for a foundation of solid cement. When the location chosen for the school was found to be solid rock, the Army blasted out the rock and filled it with cement, according to specifications.

One day as General Groves was touring around the Mesa he asked how the school was getting along. When he saw how, he blew up and fired the unfortunate major in charge on the spot and off the Mesa.

A count was made of children, apparently by slide rule, statistics of population, mean tests, and what not. No one came to the site to count noses and the age of the noses, which was important. The average age in Los Alamos was about 25, so the children were babies or yet unborn. The overcrowded nursery school was not included in the plans and had to be privately organized by Mesa mothers. Added to this miscount was the underlying assumption that the entire community would be composed of brilliant scientists who would not only have brilliant wives, but children with abnormally high IQs. But this was not in accord with facts. Only eight of the forty students in the Upper School, that first fall of 1943, were children of staff members and none of them was above average intelligence. Although all eight expected to go on to college, very few of the rest expected or even wanted to.

When school opened, late in the fall, none of the Upper School kids had a mind to settle down into formal classes five days a week. All the teenagers had roamed the Mesa the entire spring and summer and well into the fall while the school was being built. The Army had been very generous with them, loaning them trucks and jeeps for trips, and became angry only once when some kids deliberately pushed a jeep down the side of a steep canyon just for laughs. Their only punishment was a severe scolding and no use of the jeeps for a while.

These children sensed at once that the school was new and the management uncertain, and they made the most of it. They were not bad kids, except for one or two who led the pack and bragged about having been expelled from several schools. These few wielded enough influence on the group to take them all down to Santa Fe on a school day in an Army truck. I remember Alice poking her head in my door on her way home from school at noon saying, "All gone to Santa Fe again. My class has only seven: Bill and Jack, two Flanders, Joanna Jorgenson, Jean Cline and Kay Froman." Even the regular Army bus would stop long enough in Española for the teenagers to run into liquor stores for whiskey. Some of us tried to organize parties for the kids before school opened, but the gang could break up anything. The rest of the children lost interest, and we had to give up, too.

The Lower School (first to sixth grades) did not have the extreme disciplinary problems of the Upper School, but it had unusual minor problems such as lice in the heads of the first grade, which disrupted the routine for weeks. Doc Barnett went to the school every morning to go over the heads, including the teacher's. Doc taught the mothers how to hunt for lice every evening, and he ordered all heads shorn as short as possible. Mothers of little girls with golden curls wept when the locks were cut. We also had a bout with ringworm at the same time. I remember little Claudio Segré, wearing a kerchief over his shaved head, coming down our road bringing Mici's wash, which he did—for a consideration, of course—in his mother's washer. The kids would tease him and yank off his kerchief to expose his bald head with the purple ointment on it, but Claudio was a good sport about it.

Another prediction in the survey was that no extra teachers would have to be hired. It proposed that wives of the scientists and Post employees would do the teaching, but as far as I know, none of the wives was queried about her qualifications or willingness. Fortunately, a few were both qualified and willing. Alice Smith agreed to teach social sciences. Jane Wilson was a graduate in English and offered to try. Betty Inglis was experienced in teaching math, and Mrs. Long was a chemist with teaching experience. No one was available to teach any language during our years there, although we had natives of half the countries of Europe living up there and plenty of Spanish-speaking personnel. Several wives, like Peg Bainbridge, had PhDs in language, but claimed they knew no grammar and had held only graduate seminars in the colleges where they had taught. Furthermore, both Peg and Francoise Ulam had babies to look after, but we did prevail upon them to have small groups in French and Latin after school.

Except for a young technician sent over by Tech Area at one time, we were never able to get a physics teacher, but in our second year we found one for biology. It was not until after August 6, 1945, when it was arranged that all fathers of school students would give one lecture apiece, that we had physics. Our illustrious professors included Enrico Fermi, Rudolph Peierls, John Williams, Bob Brode, Julian Mack, Darol Froman, Theodore Jorgenson, Cyril Smith, Sam Allison, Bob Bacher, Moll Flanders, and Dana Mitchell. Even some without children, such as Dick Feynman, Hans Bethe and Victor Weisskopf, were willing to help out. Mrs. Long, the chemistry teacher, was the polio victim and never replaced.

Soon after Christmas, Betty Inglis, the math teacher, walked out of school after the Limburger Cheese Incident and refused to re-turn. One thing after another went wrong with her class and with the school management until that fateful Monday morning when she opened her desk drawer and found it filled with Limburger cheese left there the Friday before. When the incident was related to Oppenheimer, he said, "That school does stink, doesn't it?"

Alice and Jane stuck it out until the end of the war when we all went home. They deserve the greatest credit, for their responsibilities grew with increased enrollment and extra school activities. As a last resort, when Betty could not be replaced, I was paged over the

The Lower School did not have the extreme disciplinary problems of the Upper School—just minor problems like head lice in first grade.

intercom at T to come over to the school and hold down the math class. Although he was in a fine position to know my mathematical shortcomings, Moll, my boss, said I had better go. He said his eldest daughter, Ellen, could explain the problems to the class. So I left the peace and quiet of the Tech Area and cycled over to the school battlefield. The class was in unusually good order, and Ellen Flanders and Lloyd Williams explained the math problems that I, naturally, couldn't do. I continued this method for several days until the arrival of the new principal, who also taught math.

The first superintendent sent up by the survey people left after a short time, and it was quite a while before we could get a replacement since all applicants had to be interviewed off the Mesa, investigated and told just enough to entice them but not enough to frighten them. Meanwhile, the Lower School principal, Miss Saunders, who also had the third grade, assumed the entire responsibility. She threatened to leave unless she got help soon as the Upper School by this time was completely out of control. The authorities reluctantly agreed to hire another teacher who could add subjects like typing, art, and elementary biology. A friend of ours, Margery Crouch, was persuaded to try her hand.

Margery was a tough disciplinarian and had been successful in other difficult jobs. I did not share many of her ideas on education, but by this time our fancy ideas on education seemed beside the point. After she was interviewed and agreed to come up, I wangled one of the single apartments for her, reluctantly given for one person. I was tired of our only school being treated as a step-child by the Manhattan District.

As soon as she arrived, we had dinner at our house and then took her to her apartment. No sooner was she inside the door than the entire school board called on her. They were a bunch of desperate men who promised to back her up on any measures she saw fit to take. The latest incident had been the shooting of a large school window full of bullet holes. The culprits bragged about the feat, but the Army held the school authorities responsible and refused to discipline the boys. When the school board took Margery to visit the school that evening, she admired the view of snow covered mountains through the bullet holes.

Later that same evening, I took Margery to a party given by Mary Frankel, my overseer at T, to initiate her into Mesa social life. It was one of those muddy days, and Dick Feynman came to the party in his usual attire of unpressed white shirt, brown wool pants rolled up at the bottom and his heavy work shoes. He stood at the kitchen door with a roll of newspapers, which he carefully laid down as a path, stepping from one to the next until he got to a chair.

When Margery looked startled, he explained that he always came to parties this way. Two years later when he came to school to give a physics lecture, he wore a coat and tie, and Margery did not recognize him at first. He told her he had pressed his shirt for the occasion by laying it out still damp under his mattress and sleeping on it. His lecture was a spectacular success. He wrote equations on the blackboard with both hands at once, each making different marks with the chalk. The students were enthralled and asked for him again.

When Margery went to school for her first day, she was met by the harassed Miss Saunders, acting principal in the emergency, who took her to the largest room, which also served as an assembly hall. The Upper School was waiting in force with hostile faces and Margery was put at once on her mettle. "This is Mrs. Crouch, the new principal," Miss Saunders announced and almost ran out of the room, back to her nice little third grade.

Margery cut short her planned speech and instead asked if there were any questions. After an embarrassed silence, Lloyd Williams rose to his lanky height. He was a handsome lad of sixteen and assumed the role of spokesman. "What exactly will be your policy on unexcused absences, Mrs. Crouch?"

"Well," answered the new principal, "since you have a particular reason for asking"—and everybody laughed—"you might explain further what you have in mind." Lloyd was equal to the task. He explained how all employees in the Tech Area were allowed one half-day a week to go shopping in Santa Fe since they worked a six-day week. So, he argued, shouldn't the school have a similar privilege?

Margery remembered the tales we had told about hooky and she caught the "six-day week" phrase in Lloyd's presentation, but all she said was "I don't know yet what my policy will be but it will be adequate."

And it was. The Saturday School was instituted. Poor Alice and Jane quaked at the idea and predicted no one would show up on Saturday morning. On the following Friday, Margery read off names of those who had been absent during the week and would be "eligible" for Saturday School. Everyone eligible turned up and each was given a theme to write all morning. It was good hard work and no fun at all. After several Saturdays of this, unexcused absences ceased and playing hooky became a thing of the past—or nearly so.

Little by little, the climate changed around the school, and the children began to enjoy it. Even their manners changed. They took gum out of their mouths before reciting, wore fewer sloppy clothes and sat up straight instead of lounging with their feet on the desk. Margery made a few enemies among the Post authorities, the school board and even her best friends, but on the whole, we all supported her and were eternally grateful for her efforts.

The school did improve and it did serve the majority of the students, but it never became the dream school we expected for our children. But we got the whole Upper School under control, and that was the main problem. The new superintendent, Esther Swenson, and Margery obtained results we had not thought possible. When the town population increased, bringing many more Upper School children, it was a mercy the school had come under constructive management.

Miss Swenson soon began to talk of getting the school accredited, which some of us thought unnecessary if we thought about it at all. We had second thoughts, however, when it was pointed out that our children might not get into college or be properly transferred to other schools if we had no professional status.

One feature that shocked Margery was that no records had been kept, no attendance, no transcripts of children's previous records had been collected. She discovered that the kids had placed themselves in the grade of their own choosing, making unscrambling them a major undertaking.

It did not prove easy to get on the accredited lists. For one thing, we could not be inspected or checked on. At last it was arranged that the University of California would send up Professor Will Dennes, a former personnel director who was already cleared and knew something about accrediting. He acted as a go-between, connecting us with the outer world.

In June 1944 our first graduation class consisted of two girls, Ellen Flanders and Jean Cline, who had been accepted by the Universities of Chicago and California, respectively. In the fall of 1945 when Jean Cline at Cal let it be known for the first time that she had attended Los Alamos school, she was written up in the *Daily Cal* as the "Atomic Baby."

We had an active PTA on the Hill, although we were not affiliated with the national organization. This may have been just as well since we were rather free-wheeling in our gatherings, which often turned into town meetings to discuss any current crisis. Our group served as a money-raiser, library and social organization as well as PTA. In the summer we had wonderful potluck suppers, announced in mimeographed notices in both English and Spanish, our two official languages. We fixed up a flat picnic area with plank tables under the pines and asked each family to bring a dish typical of its nationality. The array of dishes ranged from pasta, French ribbon cakes, salad, Boston baked beans, Texas short ribs with sauce, Swedish meat balls and British steak and kidney pie. Some of the bachelors, heading for the Mess Hall around 6 P.M., would pass the families converging on the school with pungent steaming hot dishes. They begged to be included in the supper, offering to pay any price for a delicious meal. Willie Higinbotham was one of the privileged bachelors. When he was asked to sing for his supper, as he said, he brought his accordion along and lead group singing. Some of the kids had guitars and joined in to make it all a family affair.

Not all the school projects came off successfully and some had to be abandoned in a hurry. Thinking it would make the entrance to these large gatherings more accessible, Margery organized an "exercise detail" after school to clear the front yard of big stones. The kids came in old clothes and happily pitched in, huffing and puffing to re- move the boulders to one corner where they planned to make a rock garden. But as they loosened the top stones, they found as many more underneath, and the task seemed hopeless. Worse yet, the dust loosened in the process blew into the nearby houses and the tenants complained. Margery felt as guilty as the major who blasted the rock in the first place. The kids thought it was a big joke.

In May 1945, an ambitious high school revue went into rehearsal and quite a number of us were roped in to help. Elsie Tuck, a British wife, wrote and directed a ballet, I helped train dancers for several numbers, and the two Kays taught the songs, mostly composed by Jane Wilson and her English classes. Miss Swenson and Margery kept track of everything in general.

We had the usual last minute troubles. My boys didn't tell me that they had to have dark pants for each quadrille, so I quickly had to borrow a two-pants suit from a young man in the dorm and turn up the bottoms. The morning of the opening, the head ballerina had her appendix removed, and Elsie had to take her part. Jane Flanders finally consented to sing her solo after a temperamental outburst, and the show went on.

During a rehearsal the month before, as my twenty dancers were trying on the skirts they were to wear in the show, a special messenger came in and whispered to me that President Roosevelt was dead. I stopped the music, told the girls to sit down on the floor, and broke the news. The girls were stunned and speechless. I immediately dismissed them, and as I walked home with the skirts over my arm I found everyone I met in a state of shock.

We all were aware that Los Alamos was a special project of the President, and we were all personally affected. When the news came over the loudspeaker in the Tech Area, crowds gathered and everyone wondered what would become of the project now, since Truman, who would succeed to the presidency, did not know of our existence. A pall settled over our town. There was a memorial service in the theater, at which Oppenheimer spoke, and everyone was quiet and thoughtful, emotionally moved at the loss of a great man. V-E day, which came a month later, did not have the impact on our Mesa that the death of Roosevelt did.

The song at the end of the high school revue, written by Jane and her students and sung to the tune of the Marine Corps hymn, rather summed up the purpose of our town. We were united in the war effort, doing our share for victory, asked of us by the President whose loss was mourned by the world:

"From the east coast, from the west coast, and the land
that lies between
We arrived here at Los Alamos, queerest city ever seen.
Oh, we love our mountain stronghold, and our homes
among the stars.
It's the strangest story ever told, this mesa town of ours.
From the plains of neighbor Texas and the sidewalks of
New York
We arrived here at Los Alamos to learn, to play, to work.
We have vision strong to guide us, proud form of liberty.
Whatever is denied us is all for liberty."

When Margery Crouch took her first vacation to California in the summer of 1945, she happened to be visiting a Girl Scout camp on August 6 when the news of the Hiroshima bomb reached the camp. The scout leaders called a special service of prayer that evening around the campfire. During the service a prayer was said for the victims of the A-bomb and also for the unfortunate people at Los Alamos who had constructed the terrible weapon. Margery, of course, had not mentioned where she was living since it was top secret when she left the site. She had not known what the project was making, either, so she suffered a shock. She felt it prudent to leave next day without saying a word about her association. She was dismayed to realize that our patriotic contribution to the war effort could be regarded in this light.

8 Mesa Business

"Mesa business" was the term we used for community affairs, as distinguished from private parties. We knew we were to be completely self-contained for the years at Los Alamos. No outside contacts were allowed, unless Edith Warner and Dorothy McKibbin can be regarded as exceptions, and whatever recreation or fun we had, had to be provided by ourselves.

In our first year we organized everybody and everything. I'm sure we overdid it in our first flush of enthusiasm, and we overrated some of our talents. There was no formal organization, no committee appointed by Oppenheimer, Post authorities, or anyone else. "Mesa business" was everyone's business, and an activity was born when anyone had an idea and pushed it through.

It was surprisingly easy to set up group activities. I suppose it was because we had no competition from outside affairs. Families coming to Los Alamos were considered for abilities that would enrich our lives. Every time a new family was due to arrive, word got around as to their assets for the community good. Could they sing? Could they dance? What were they bringing up? We assigned their services and possessions even before we knew their names. When we heard Joe Hirschfelder's mother was coming without encumbrances to fill her days, we were certain she could be counted on as a baby sitter. When she was tactfully sounded out on this, her answer was forthright. "I can't see taking care of other people's children. I always had a nurse for Joe and his sister, don't you know."

Just when the orchestra was struggling to keep alive, the grapevine buzzed with the news of the impending arrival of a family with an eleven-piece dining set and a harp. Moll Flanders, who led the orchestra, immediately counted on the harp. As for the harpist, Moll reasoned, "Surely no one would bring a harp up this road unless he or she played it." The eleven-piece dining set would have to take its place in the general GI storeroom we all used, along with Doty Seymour's power lawn mower, several Persian rugs of sizes exceeding the dimensions of living rooms, and other relics of the past. It turned out that the harp family was sent to Oak Ridge.

During the first summer there was a temporary Post social committee that organized several public affairs. The first was a Sadie Hawkins Day party with a program of entertainment in the theater, after which everyone went to the PX for beer or Cokes. The show included songs by Spanish girls, dances by a San Ildefonso Indian, and many other features.

Our square-dance group gave a demonstration of one square. There were prizes for various categories, and before I knew what was happening, I was pushed out on the stage to receive our group's prize, a live and squawking chicken. The tremendous applause was solely at my expense, for it was only too obvious that the chicken and I were terrified of each other. Afterward, we retired to the PX, and there we sat, taking turns holding the chicken and drinking beer from bottles, neither of which I had ever done before. I remember Mrs. Hirschfelder, just arrived on the Hill, was utterly delighted at this sample of life on the site.

We took the hen home and boxed it up on our end of the kitchen porch. Although there were no rules against keeping barnyard fowl, we thought it best to eat the hen as soon as possible. My Indian half-day killed and dressed it while we were away, and I invited the dance square to come and share the tough, skinny bird that provided only a morsel apiece. Later on there was a Mesa circus with everyone contributing acts and food to sell to provide funds for the school play equipment. I remember in particular Mrs. Gonzales' sopaipilla factory in her tiny kitchen in one of the log houses opposite the Commissary. On her stove she had a very large black iron kettle of smoking hot fat into which she dropped bits of dough that came out hollow brown balls. Mr. Gonzales and his helpers split them open, put honey in the hollow as fast as they were cooked, and sold them piping hot to a long line of customers who gobbled them on the spot. The news spread to the dorms and hungry men came running. The sopaipillas made the most money.

Since most of the Mesa children were nursery-school age, one of the first organized efforts was a pre-school group. The Army built them a large green house and fenced in a dusty yard. Some of the early residents, like Elsie McMillan, Jim Nolan, Sally Hawkins, Schatsie Davis and others, were able to buy the best equipment while the Army was still feeling extremely generous. The equipment investment was well worth the expense, for the nursery school was one of our largest institutions and, as far as I heard, in capable hands. I used to hear about the long waiting list made up of babies registered as soon as Jim Nolan delivered them to PO Box 1663.

When we arrived in September, the social groups for youngsters also were thriving. Martha Parsons had Girl Scouts the age of her Peggy. There was a Cub Scout den, and boys under ten were gathered into a new outfit, Buds, by a most enterprising young wife, Gracia Hane. Because boys this age seemed most uncivilized, Gracia was regarded as going well beyond the call of duty when twice a week she drained off a dozen or more of the six, seven, and eight year olds, including Stevie Smith and Mike Hane, who were usually up to something in front of our house.

Dorothy Hillhouse, who taught second grade when school opened, had a Brownie group, and by the end of the summer the little girls had learned to dance exceedingly well and were often invited to perform at community functions. The little girls did so well that I got an idea one morning as I gazed on our street scene and pondered that telephone pole in the middle of the open space in a town where there were no telephones. I remembered the Maypole festivals of my child- hood and visualized the little girls winding pink and white streamers fastened to the silly pole. Dorothy liked my ideas, so I bought the cloth in Santa Fe and tore it into strips. Then I went to see the major. How would he feel about tacking my pink and white ribbons to his telephone pole for a Maypole dance, I asked him. He looked at me for a moment and his patient sigh plainly asked, "What next, for Heaven's sake? These people are a bit fey up here." He refused the use of the telephone pole but magnanimously offered to erect another pole I chose.

A soldier put up a slender pole in a flat place near the Big House, and my husband made a disc for the streamers that could be taken down at night. On our first practice day, the little girls got into a hopeless tangle, compounded by the raw edges of the streamers torn in the wind, so I had to hem all the ribbons. Most of the children

The first Maypole dance was a pretty sight with little girls in long skirts and flowers in their hair skipping in time to phonograph music.

had never even seen a Maypole before, and I had great difficulties with them in the simplest weaving patterns. But the day finally arrived, duly announced in the *Daily Bulletin*. It was a pretty sight with the girls in long full skirts, flowers in their hair, and their little feet keeping time with the music from our wind-up phonograph. The audience was composed mostly of mothers with babies, workmen going along the roads, and a number of young dorm men, attracted by the music carried all over the Mesa by the wind from the mountains. Dorothy's second grade continued the first-of-May tradition for many years.

We had a Little Theater group, made up mostly of younger people, that presented a play every so often. Performances were in the theater, but rehearsals were held all over the Mesa—in dorm common rooms with people coming and going, outdoors under the trees with an uninvited audience, and in the Mess Hall. Our theater

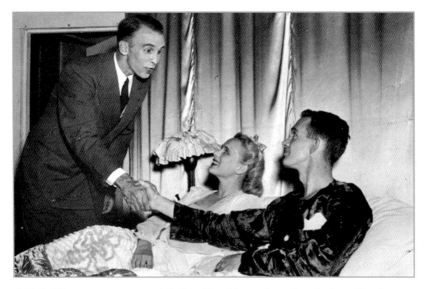

A Little Theater group presented plays like this one from time to time. Nearly everyone was asked to help in some way so that every performance was assured of an appreciative and capacity audience.

was used constantly from early morning until late at night for gym classes for soldiers and the school, exhibits, dances, movies, meetings, church and other gatherings.

Little publicity was needed for a forthcoming play. Nearly everyone on the Mesa had been part of the rehearsal, been approached for props, or been asked to help out in some way, so every performance was assured of an appreciative and capacity audience.

After the play, it was the custom for the players to come out in grease paint and be congratulated by their public. Then we pushed back the chairs and benches and danced until midnight to music often provided by Mr. Olmstead's jazz band.

One of our biggest hits was "Arsenic and Old Lace" with Betty Brixner as the old lady. Betty was a pretty blonde of twenty-five, so she had a good deal of acting to do but carried it off very well. The sets were designed by David Anderson, who assembled them, as "Victorian GI" with bits of lace, flowered bedspreads, and velvet capes draped over the familiar GI imitation leather furniture everyone knew so well. The picture of "dear Father" was painted at the last moment on someone's back porch and dripped visibly the first night of the show.

The high spot of the show was the end of the last act when the dead bodies were brought up from the cellar. It was kept top-secret so well that the audience was unprepared to see Oppenheimer brought up stiff as a corpse and laid on the floor, then Deak Parsons, then Bob Bacher, Cyril Smith, Harold Agnew and others. Cyril Smith remarked on the way home that it was the most restful occupation he had on the Mesa.

Although my efforts to run a dance group at the school had failed, the adult square dance group thrived at all times. When we arrived on the Mesa, it was going strong with the two butchers, George and Mack, in charge. It was held in the theater, which was barren and uncomfortable with only four or six squares. The Lodge was off limits for dancing, apparently because the housekeeper, whom the Army had inherited with the building, preferred peace and quiet in her large rooms and didn't want her doors and walls scuffed up. Despite our efforts, it was not until Oppie heard our tales of woe that we were notified the Lodge was available, $5 an evening. The housekeeper stayed the first few times to see how careful we were, but we never succeeded in getting her to dance with us. In the large and pleasant atmosphere of the Lodge, more and more dancers came to join us until we filled the long dining room to overflowing and had two squares set up in the hall.

We danced couple dances, too—schottisches, polkas, waltzes, la raspa and many others—with music provided by our pooled records. In our western dance costumes—cowboy boots, jeans and bright shirts for the men, long full dresses with several petticoats for the women— we got hot and thirsty in the dry desert air. Because the chronic shortage of women meant a shortage of partners, the men could sit and rest occasionally, but we women had to keep going.

One month we heard tales that another caller of squares was due to arrive—the incomparable Willie Higinbotham with his accordion, or "Stomach Steinway." His reputation as a firebrand seemed exaggerated when we first saw this quiet, serious, unassuming little man who was so shy we had to plead with him to join us. But once he got up at the end of the long room and let loose with his beloved accordion, electric sparks went over the Lodge. His voice and timing inspired greater hilarity, and the shouts and twirling increased until it was time to leave the Lodge at 12:00 sharp.

The time came when we could squeeze no more squares into the Lodge, and we reluctantly moved to the Mess Hall, a much larger floor space better for our fast waltzes and polkas. It became increasingly hard for George to keep order in so many squares, but Willie could out shout any disorder. He said the bigger, the mob the better he liked it.

We began meeting one hour earlier to teach newcomers. Among others, the Fermi family—Enrico, Laura, and daughter Nella —came but only sat and watched. Finally the two women were persuaded to try, but Enrico sat tight, intensely studying the movements. He said in his mild and reasonable voice he would let me know when he was ready to join a square, and one could almost see his mind watching and remembering. Then one evening he came up to me and said, "Well, I think I am ready now, if you will be my partner." He offered to be head couple, which I thought most unwise for his first venture, but I could do nothing about it, and the music began. He led me out on the exact beat, knew exactly each move to make and when. He never made a mistake then or thereafter. I wouldn't say he enjoyed himself, for he was so intent on not making a mistake, which the best of us did all the time. Although I congratulated him, I also kidded him and admonished him to relax and have fun. He laughed tolerantly, but I knew he would continue to dance with his brains instead of his feet.

Another physicist, Dick Feynman, came one evening to see what this square dancing was all about and was caught up in the excitement at once. He joined in a square immediately, and we all pushed him into the right places at the right times, but after it was over he said he was never so confused in his life. "It's too hard, much too hard, I can't learn, I'll never learn," he complained and threw up his hands in despair. His feet could act, however, and he went into polkas and waltzes naturally, just following the music and letting go.

We also had slower dances with softer music. Willie taught us an intricate Swedish reel with plaintive languid music from his accordion. It was perfect to end an evening, but he said it was too moody, and he wouldn't put us through it often. Perhaps this expressed a general reaction in our town—an instinctive knowledge that vigorous gaiety must be our tenor, and that we perhaps could not afford much emotional content and contemplation.

We had a good deal of music at Los Alamos, organized and unorganized. Walking along the roads in the evening we heard the strains of Bach or Mozart that filled the air. High up in the mountains, radio reception was poor, but we had our own station in the last year. It advertised in the Bulletin for records from Mesa collections, which were quite extensive, and our otherwise quiet mesa was soon saturated with the world's best music.

We had quite a few very good musicians on the Hill who were able to present concerts open to the Mesa public. Sometimes we charged a fee and used the proceeds for some local "charity"— school equipment, cement for a swimming pool, etc. Otto Frisch and Winifred Moon of the British Mission both gave concerts for piano and violin. Several young wives gave piano recitals, and Willie Higinbotham and Fred Reines had a barbershop group. Busy as they were, everyone was quite willing to contribute what talent he or she had. There was a lot of chamber music, and little informal gatherings met in almost every neighborhood for practice.

There were two organized singing groups, a small one and a large chorus. The smaller group comprised twelve invited singers selected by Kay Manley for their blending qualities. Kay and Elinor Ramsay sang soprano; Kay Anderson, Schatsie Davis, and Sally Dow sang contralto; David Anderson and my husband sang bass; and several SED boys sang tenor, along with Robert Dike when he arrived on the Hill. They prepared two concerts at the Lodge—one Christmas carols and one Easter music. Both concerts would have done justice to any professional singers.

The Mesa Chorus, a large singing group open to everyone who wanted to sing, was run by the Flanders, with Moll conducting and either Sally or Harold Boaz on the piano. The chorus gave Handel's *Messiah* each year and other popular oratorios. The first *Messiah* at the Lodge had about fifty voices: with solo voices that had all been at least partly professional. It was a superb performance—so good that it set a standard for all future recitals.

Some of us remembered the first performance of the *Messiah* not only for the excellence of the concert, but because Willie. Higinbotham, with his fine tenor voice, came in a moment too soon after the renowned pause in the "Hallelujah Chorus," shattering the dramatic silence of the Lodge. Poor Willie never lived it down. It was said the story even followed him to Washington where he went to lobby for civilian control of atomic energy late in 1945. After the concert, Otto Frisch congratulated Willie. "I've heard the *Messiah* perhaps some thirty times in my life," he said, "and I've always waited for someone to come in too soon. It was very satisfying to me."

The first Christmas, when our community was smaller and more homogeneous than it later became, Moll's chorus packed into the back of an Army truck and sang Christmas carols as they slowly rode around the town. Everyone came out their doors on the clear, starry night to listen and wish the singers a merry Christmas. The carolers resembled an old fashioned Christmas card, with their bright red and green and white caps and mufflers. It was a lovely holiday season that first year, with a deep blanket of snow to keep our water pipes warm and snug. Our spirits soared with hopes for an early ending of the war, to be helped by our efforts. The stolid white mountains surrounding our town seemed to speak of a possible enduring peace on earth. Meanwhile, our warm houses were jolly with Christmas cheer.

Hikes into Bandelier National Monument, where lectures and tours were offered, were popular Sunday activities.

9 Sunday Trips and Sports

Sunday trips were taken rather seriously in our town. The General himself urged us to "get off the Mesa" once a week. He insisted we be issued "B" gas-ration coupons for this purpose. We walked or rode bicycles around the town for the most part, so all our gas was saved for excursions on Sunday, our one day off. The factory whistle did not blow on Sunday, and it was regarded as unsporting to sneak over to the Technical Area to get in some work.

Once off the Mesa, outside the gates, the whole vast area of mountains, valleys, and mesas was open to us. We could have gotten away from each other as well, but we usually took our trips with other families, filling each car with bachelors or lone school teachers. We planned some Sundays at the last moment, asking whomever was close at hand. Small fry were dispatched to dorms, the Big House, and the Lodge to summon anyone to fill up a car going wherever was planned for the day. There was no civilian Sunday traffic to buck on our trips, and we could even walk to picnic places if we chose. Few tourists came to our favorite haunts in wartime. We came to regard the whole region as our own, and if we met strangers, we looked upon them as trespassers.

Even Bandelier National Monument, with its ancient ruins, was all but deserted until we came on the scene. The lodge and museum were closed for the duration, with a lone ranger left in charge. He welcomed us with open arms, and built a fire for us in the museum stone hearth when it was chilly.

We were careful at first not to mention whence we came, but the ranger began to call us by name, although we never signed his visitors book. Perhaps he was one of the network of people said to be keeping an eye on us when we left the Mesa, but we never knew. He arranged special lectures and tours through the ruins on certain Sundays, and these were announced in the *Daily Bulletin*. All the school grades had their turn in the park, arriving in Army buses for anthropological field trips. Sometimes entire divisions from the Technical Area had picnics at Bandelier.

One Sunday we brought a new British couple, Philip and Winifred Moon, for a quiet stroll through the ruins, but as we parked just on the edge of the entrance, we heard the unmistakable strains of Willie's voice and accordion, ringing down the ancient canyon. He was there all right, with his gang from the electronics division, two hundred strong, trying to form squares on the ancient terrain. Poor Winifred Moon—she had wanted to get away from the "hectivity" that she found so oppressing at Los Alamos. The sun was very hot as we climbed higher in the ruins to get away from Willie and his gang, and Winifred soon wilted. All the British colony tended to collapse in the desert heat. It was the one feature at Los Alamos that always defeated them. I saved the day when we crawled into a deep cave to sip the tea we had brought along.

Alice and I went to Bandelier one Saturday with a carload of children, and while they ran about, we sat and talked with the ranger. He told us fascinating facts about the ruins before they became a national monument in the early 1900's and before New Mexico became a state. The ancient Indian ruins had many invasions, he said, by bandits and fugitives from justice who lived for years in the caves. Someday, he told us, he would write the story of the latest invasion by "you from the Pajarito Plateau, who are so full of life and do modernistic war dancing on the ancient ground where the Indians pounded their bare feet in ceremonial dances."

Another haunt of ours was the Valle Grande, a huge caldera high up in the Jemez Mountains. After we left the project's West Gate, the dirt road wound and twisted up and up until suddenly the vast valley came into view. In cold weather we drove up with chains on the tires and built huge fires to keep warm while we ate lunch. This was another of our "private" show places, to which we could proudly bring newcomers.

Peg Bainbridge once organized a picnic to show the Chadwicks, newly arrived to head the British Mission, one of our finest American scenes. We fixed a very elegant repast with tablecloth, cocktails, and dishes of hot food laid out on the rustic table near the frozen stream. Sir James and Lady Chadwick were rather formidable and stern-appearing and had decided views on America. They tended to regard Los Alamos as a typical American community. After our more than adequate meal, the men went off for a hike, discussing science as they went, and we wives huddled by the open fire to gossip. Over coffee and cigarettes we discussed Anglo-American relations and pointed out the many misconceptions. Peg felt rewarded for her efforts, convinced that Lady Chadwick, who had not been to the States before, now realized that there was much more to this country than her countrymen knew.

Some of our rougher souls jeered at picnics with tablecloths and preferred to set out with sandwiches in pocket to hike long distances or climb over uncataloged Indian ruins that could be found in every mesa cliff on the entire Pajarito Plateau. Most of our foreign-born preferred scenery to ruins, much to the dismay of Helen Allison who had studied the local anthropology and thought it compared favorably with other parts of the world. Since our ruins were ancient, authentic and most picturesque in setting, what more could be expected of any ruins, Helen demanded of the detractors. She posed this question to Italians Emilio Segré and Enrico Fermi in her most severe manner, and the only answer they could find was that they just preferred fish and mushrooms on Sundays.

Emilio also got a severe scolding from Helen when she discovered that his favorite mushroom grounds, where he gathered paper bags full of tiny button fungi, was situated just below the rock cliff where one of the best plumed serpent petroglyph can be seen when the shadows fall. Emilio had never noticed it, nor looked to see the many other rock carvings. Enrico said the live Indians intrigued him more than the dead ones.

There was peace and quiet in the open country around our Mesa, but as time went on, more and more canyons and mesas were closed off for testing. Notices were put in the *Daily Bulletin* to this effect. We complained that the Technical Area was expanding into ancient unspoiled land, with installations appearing in place of wind-sculpted pines and shrubs and richly colored rocks. Quonset huts, shamelessly erected in front of cliff dwellings and manned by gun-bearing soldiers, barred entrance to nature lovers. No one listened to us, and we had to go farther and farther from home base to get away from it all. This was "progress" with a special vengeance.

It was an easy hike to picnic places like this one in Omega Canyon.

There were plenty of streams for fishing and generous gifts of fish were passed around on Sunday evenings. As Emilio used to say to newcomers, "The streams are full of big trout. All you have to do is throw a line and they bite you, even if you are shouting." Hunting also was good. Venison dinners were popular in our town, and we ate Emilio's mushrooms and bunches of fresh watercress from the upper Rio Grande.

A few of the energetic young men found the ancient Shrine of the Stone Lions, two mountain lions carved into the tuff, which is nearly inaccessible on a distant Bandelier mesa. Tales of their trip intrigued Genia Peierls, a Russian-born British subject, whose husband Rudy had become head of the British Mission, and made her determined to "conquer the Stone Lions" along with me. Although the ranger warned that trails were not well marked, we planned a Sunday trip to find the legendary carvings.

Unable to stir up much enthusiasm, we recruited a more or less captive party. Genia commandeered three young bachelors recently arrived in the British Mission who knew nothing of the desert trips; I had a carload of young Navy ensigns, fresh from basic training, who came to work with my husband. So we started out with our amenable guests in our Ford with the Peierls in "Conky," the 1925 Nash they had bought in Santa Fe. The Nash got one mile farther into the brush where we started our hike than our Ford, a feat I greatly appreciated on the return. Genia was firm about "taking along no sissies," but scoffed when I was equally firm about carrying liquids in the desert country. Neither of our husbands was convinced there were any lions in the first place, and both doubted we would reach them if there were. Some six miles of rocky, uncertain trail sounded ominous. Genia snorted when she saw our stout walking shoes. She wore tennis shoes and no socks. "Best for stones, best for bunions," she said. She set a fast walking pace, getting well ahead, then waiting for the rest of us, and she would not allow us to eat our sandwiches until the second canyon. She said we must go on, and her young men followed, albeit a bit pale from the altitude.

Our Navy crew, having made a number of snide remarks about the absence of cross-country desert treks from their basic training were happily bathing their feet in the cool mountain stream and were quite comfortable staying right where they were. Genia took the hint and said, "OK, we proceed to Stone Lions without the U.S. Navy. All aboard." The boys promised to wait for us, or to tell the authorities if we did not return. We started up again, Genia well in advance. The Brtishers kept up with their hostess, being much too shy to buck her pace. We went over two more mesas before we found the Stone Lions half buried among the brush. Genia looked a bit glum, and her loud voice carried far and wide from the highest spot on the mesa, "House cats only my dear. Not well made and maybe not even old." I had read about the sacred beasts, however, and I was thrilled. Besides that, the view was superb. One could see all the other mesas and the Rio Grande in the far canyon below.

On the way back the young men recently arrived from England looked out over the wide expanse of desert region and the ribbon of water shining in the setting sun. One of them, dark and slim, wearing tortoise-shell-rimmed glasses, spoke in his soft voice with a slight German accent, "I have not seen New York, nor Chicago, but I have seen the Stone Lions." He smiled pleasantly as we walked on. His name was Klaus Fuchs. (In 1950, Fuchs was convicted as a spy.)

Besides picnics, fishing, and hunting ruins, there were fiestas and Indian ceremonial dances to attend. We went to all of them and on Sundays when the men could join us. Occasionally we could persuade men to knock off on Saturday afternoon to attend something special, such as the Santa Fe Fiesta. When the Indians discovered their dances were much better attended if held on Sundays, they switched some of them. Like other performers, the Indians loved a good audience, and I think they liked a good attendance from their friends at Los Alamos.

We were a good audience—enthusiastic and uncritical. We came to have a good time and brought all the kids. Most of our people did not know one ceremonial dance from another, but they liked the liveliness of the show, and they loved to take pictures.
We have been much criticized by local anthropologists, who have said the influence of Los Alamos on the Indians' traditional culture has been corrupting. If so, we didn't do it on purpose. We just enjoyed the Indians and what they had to offer, just as they enjoyed our Hill life and drinking Cokes in our PX.

Any Sunday Feast Day at one of the nearby pueblos would find a large crowd from the Hill, being personally greeted by Indians we knew, such as Tilano who lived at Miss Warner's at Otowi Bridge. He was very stern-looking on Feast Days. He brusquely forbade tourists to take photos while slyly encouraging us to do so, and took great interest in the results that we brought down to Miss Warner's to show him.

Our first San Ildefonso Feast Day, which is in January, was memorable for the mud. It was extremely cold when some of us went down at dawn to see the early ceremonials, then had breakfast at Rosalie's house in the pueblo. It was the first time I tasted the round loaves of bread that are made in the beehive ovens. By the middle of the day, when the Comanche war dance was going strong in the pueblo plaza, the strong sun caused a thaw that turned the snow and the ground beneath it into foot-deep mud. The poor dancers slipped and slid and our children were covered with wet mud.

How magnificent the men looked in painand war feathers! We hardly recognized our furnace stokers, caretakers and technicians of week-day life. We learned that to sew the feathers together for the

War Dance takes so much time that the dance is not given often. Our Indian friends implied that they staged it particularly for us that year. Our children were delighted to see little Tony Martinez, who lived on the site in a greenhouse and went to nursery school, dancing with his father Popovi Da. They were dressed in feathers like the rest, and Tony maintained the intricate rhythm although he was very young. His grandmother, Maria, the potter, looked very proud of both her son and grandson. Po, who was in the Army, wore his khaki uniform at his job in T.

The annual Santa Fe Fiesta comes for three days in September. Everyone wore fiesta costumes, but since we were not supposed to take part or mingle with people unnecessarily, we wore ordinary clothes. As a result, we were more conspicuous than if we had dressed up, which we learned to do later. It was just such innocent non-conformities as this that enabled Santa Fe to identify people from the Hill. We didn't know Santa Fe people, but we knew many of the Indians sitting around the plaza. All during Fiesta week, our maid service had dwindled so that our houses were uncleaned, and mothers had to stay home from work in some cases. So here were all the maids, sitting placidly on the wide sidewalk with trinkets, pottery, moccasins, baskets and jewelry spread out around them to tempt tourists. In front of the Palace of the Governors, we met Montoya, head caretaker at the Big House, swaggering along in extra gay finery, his long braids freshly wound with colored yarns and a fine old blanket thrown carelessly over his shoulder. He was loaded with heavy silver and turquoise jewelry, several concho belts, necklaces, and huge bracelets.

One of our bachelors recognized Montoya. "Look who is coming—our keeper of the Big House, and all dressed up and playing Indian for all he is worth."

Montoya stopped, shook hands all around, and said, "Hello, my folks, you enjoy Fiesta OK?' He looked as if he were enjoying secrets, which he was, for he had the magic pass in his pocket that got him past the MPs and into our mysterious town.

We were asked to keep out of crowded restaurants if possible, so four carloads planned a joint picnic the Saturday evening of Fiesta. We found a hill overlooking the lights just coming on in Santa Fe below us. All the rows of luminarias on the roof ledges were being lit, which made the city where we did our mundane shopping by day resemble a mysterious dream land. We dozed on the way home, and were roused by the MPs at our gate where we stopped to fish for our passes. As we entered our unromantic Army town of ugly installations and barracks and greenhouses, Alice and my husband began to sing "Home, Sweet Home."… "Be it ever so humble there's no place like home…."

We had winter sports of all kinds. There was sledding and kindergarten-slope skiing right on our Mesa for the children, skating on a pond near the town, and skiing for experts in the easily accessible mountains.

The pond, down in a pleasant canyon, had been used for skating by the Ranch School in winter. It froze over early in the year and the Army cleaned it off as best they could without an ice-scraping machine. The soldiers put up a shed, made a barbecue pit for a big fire, and supplied it with plenty of cut wood. It was a lovely spot by day or evening, and on cold frosty nights everyone came who could find a pair of skates. But the rough ice was never very good for skating, at least for those of us brought up in indoor rinks. The pond was never level, a very queer experience when trying to execute figure eights. Moll Flanders set up a class for advanced figures, but it was too difficult on uneven ice. Figure skating was out of the question, although I usually had a following of little girls begging me to teach them how to "go around with one foot in the air."

Martha Parsons and I got our husbands to buy figure skates on one of their trips to Washington so they could come to the pond when they were in town. Because Bob and Deak were both big men we had the problem of getting them from the hut, where the skates were put on, down the runway to the ice. Our children helped the two men, made helpless by the skates, while everyone stopped to watch. There was no rail around the pond, but a soldier put a bench at one end of the ice for Deak. Once safely there, neither man would budge. There they sat, polite and freezing. Eventually we got them on their feet, but still they wouldn't move. Bob, who had been on a rink twice, was braver and actually tried to get around the pond, but someone bumped into him and he went down, cracking the ice

The skating pond, in a pleasant canyon, was a lovely spot by day or evening, and on cold, frosty nights everyone came who could find a pair of skates.

in all directions. Totally discouraged after watching so many willing helpers try so hard to get Bob on his slippery feet, Deak was further immobilized on the bench where he remained for the entire evening. (This was the man who, with his own hands, put the first atomic bomb together in flight, before the Enola Gay, the plane carrying the bomb to Hiroshima, reached the target area.)

There were all grades of slopes suitable for skiing just a short distance from the West Gate, but one medium steep run was selected to be cleared for skiers, and at the bottom a Quonset hut provided shelter. We placed some poles for a slalom run, and many people also took off for cross-country treks. On Sundays, the slopes, like the pond, were crowded with all ages. We never managed a ski tow, but George Kistiakowsky borrowed a snow tractor from the Army to take skiers up for their downhill runs. There were always too many trees, too many children and inexpert sportsmen for good runs, but we had fun in the snow, building big fires and having hot picnic lunches. We had above-average snowfall our first two winters, and many families went out just to enjoy the fresh white country snow and to build snowmen and try out snowshoes.

Horseback riding became the chief sport of many families. The Army used the former school stables, and rented the horses or boarded private horses. Early residents who commenced a horse-buying spree were allowed to visit nearby ranches to make their purchases. The Parsons had two black mounts, Dolly and Diamond, and nearly every afternoon, Martha and ten-year-old Peggy would ride by my window on their way out to the next canyon. The Oppenheimers rode their own horses, the Flanders rented mounts, and many others had horses. A number of tales came in about wild rides, lost saddles, runaway horses the Army had to retrieve and so forth.

There were so many things to do that nearly everyone left the site for at least a part of every Sunday, summer and winter. We were situated in the middle of some of the finest vacation land in the U.S.A., and during wartime, it was quite literally all ours.

10 Social Events

Parties, both big and brassy and small and cheerful, were an integral part of Mesa life. It was a poor Saturday night that some large affair was not scheduled, and there were usually several of them. Since the factory whistle blew at 7:30 on six mornings a week, evenings other than Saturday were devoted to quiet dinners, meetings, music, movies or at homes with the kids and neighbors. On Saturdays we raised whoopee, on Sundays we took trips, the rest of the week we worked. The movies were so new, we had not heard anything about them, so most of the scientists seldom went. Neither did we read much during those hectic years, although some of us were great readers in normal times.

The biggest and brassiest parties were undoubtedly the dorm parties, so called because one entire dormitory of young men gave the party. Invitations were mimeographed on sheets of typing paper and put into the mail cubbyholes. There were always too many people, too much noise, and too much liquor, but we always had a wonderful time and looked forward to the next one before we had recovered from the last. The parties lasted until dawn, with a few diehards staying on, too lethargic to get home. By Monday morning everyone had recovered, and I never heard any tales that anyone missed coming to work on Monday.

To prepare for a dorm party, the boys took out all furniture from the common rooms to make room for dancing. The rooms were not large, so they were always crowded. One built-in bench was used for records and the record player. One dorm had a piano on which Ernie Titterton of the British Mission often played jazz. All the dorm rooms were left open for the party, an unwritten custom but rather strictly adhered to. Groups sat in the rooms when tired of dancing and discussed—or cussed—topics of the day. The party rallying point was the center hallway landing where the punch bowl dominated the scene. This was a huge clear plastic chemistry lab fixture, about five feet in diameter, brought over from the Tech Area for the party.

Ernie Titterton of the British Mission, at the piano here, often played jazz at the big, brassy dorm parties. His wife, Peg, stands at his left shoulder.

Punch-making began with a large hunk of ice, wangled, I suppose, from the Mess Hall or PX, and lowered into the plastic bowl. Then several dorm hosts started opening bottles of whatever the committee had been able to get in Santa Fe, and poured the contents over the ice. Someone would call for fruit juice for style, I imagine, and one or two small cans of juice would be added. That was the hardy punch, often with all kinds of mixed liquor in the one bowl. When the level of the bowl got low, more bottles were emptied in with another hunk of ice, but they always ran out of fruit juice first. Despite such wicked punch, there was very little, if any, unseemly behavior. As Hans Staub was fond of saying as he settled himself in one chair in one room for the evening, "Thees place ees too schmall for that kind of thing. Everyone can see if you misbehave, so eet ess not posseeble, that's all there ess to it."

Some people tried to entertain formally as far as could be managed under our slum conditions. Mary Mack thought it more civilized to serve finger bowls with fine linen, and to teach her children to serve properly. The Flanders, on the other hand, defied all convention if at all possible. Sally put food on the table in black cooking kettles, and Moll, being a gentleman of the old school, served from the kettles as if they were elegant silver dishes. If there weren't enough chairs, some sat on the floor without apology or remark. I had a caller once, a newcomer, who left calling cards on the kitchen sink when I was not at home. Impressed by such an unusual costume, little Annie Smith reported later that the caller wore gloves and a hat.

Many of our small dinners had an international flavor, in food and in conversation. One time the Italian Rossi family entertained especially for Enrico Fermi, who was not living on the Hill at the time. After a fine dinner of Italian dishes, Enrico asked why some of us didn't organize a serious discussion group to hash over post-war settlements and questions of that kind. We spent the evening making an outline of nationalities and topics and taking notes for future reference. As I read from those notes, I find some very strange ideas and predictions were voiced, along with some amusing comments.

One evening the three Italian families—Rossis, Fermis, and Segrés—were disagreeing about the future of Italian colonies conquered by Mussolini. Enrico was laying down his solutions in his usual tone of finality, when Nora Rossi broke in and questioned his judgment.

"Enrico, why do you think you know so much more than other Italians about our colonies?" she asked

Quick as a flash he answered, "Why because I am the only Italian to win the Nobel Prize in Physics."

Everyone laughed so long at this sally—intended as one or not—that the question was not resumed at that time.

Another example of a party in a small apartment was one involving sixty dinner guests. Kay Anderson, who sang solos in our musicals and taught music in the school, was of Swedish descent. She invited her friends for a smorgasbord supper that she and some friends assembled in authentic fashion. There were more than fifty-five dishes, a few sent from her home in Minnesota, but most of them made the previous week in her apartment. A list was posted on the door so everyone would know what to expect. Guests, invited for staggered hours, came and went all evening. As we entered, the tiny kitchen was filled with helpers replenishing the fifty-five dishes, and baby Christopher was calmly sitting in his highchair, being fed one can of baby food after another by anyone willing to take on the job. In the living room, a long table, covered with a lace tablecloth and dishes of food, was placed across one end, blocking the front door. The rest of the room had a row of chairs in a semicircle, filled with people eating from heaped plates. Other guests were lined up to go by the table to fill up their plates. By the time they were ready to sit, those in chairs would be ready to go to the table again or, if finished, to go home. It was an unforgettable repast.

The Bainbridge house had a real bathtub, one of the few on the Mesa. During a party a pretty young wife bet $5 that no one would dare take a bath then and there. But a young man came forward to take her up on the bet. When he discovered the door to the bathroom had no lock, he borrowed a pair of Ken's trunks, drew a tub full of hot water and prepared to soak in comfort, but of course, everyone crowded in as witnesses, offering to scrub his back and wash behind his ears. When a couple of not-entirely-sober friends tried to climb in, too, the water started to run into the hall, and Peg put a stop to the fun.

A number of guests, whose identity remained top-secret, hung around until dawn one time to arrange several dozen empty liquor bottles beside the front door of the stone house where George Kistiakowsky lived. A large sign was placed over the bottles, "Milkman, only two quarts today, please." George could be counted on to sleep on Sundays when all early churchgoers would pass by his house. George was quite angry about the prank, and no one confessed to it. However, the next Monday morning, the Bainbridge family could not get out either door, as huge piles of logs had been banked against them. Ken had to climb out a window to go to work. It seems boys will be boys, even when they grow up to be atomic scientists.

Kitty Oppenheimer had several small parties, usually just old friends from Berkeley and some of her neighbors. With her part-time job and then her new baby, she never had time to attempt large all-inclusive parties. Martha Parsons, on the other hand, liked to entertain, and I suppose felt the Navy tradition should be maintained. I discovered the hard way that a Navy cocktail invitation really means a whole meal lasting well into the evening. Before a Parsons party, Bob and I ate early with the boys before walking across the path to the Parsons' house. When we arrived, the dining room table was set out with turkey, ham, hot rolls and everything else for a buffet supper. We spent the whole evening, sitting or standing, with a highball in one hand, a plate of food in the other. Then ice cream and cake and coffee were served. Lois Bradbury continued this form of supper party when Norris, also a Navy man, became director of the Laboratory.

Fuller Lodge could be rented at $5 an evening, so group parties were often held there. One of the first groups to use the Lodge was the theoretical physicists, who offered entertainment in the form of a floor show, setting a standard for the future. Nick Metropolis, who claimed he was a member of the official magician's society, performed tricks in professional style. It was a slick show and as he steadfastly refused to divulge any secrets, some of the guests were frustrated for days trying to figure out the principles involved. There was a quiz show with questions from the floor and someone "picked at random" to answer. The first was, "The General wants to know whether the whistle blows at 7:00 or 7:30 in the morning?" Edward Teller was called up to answer. This brought thunderous applause as everyone knew about his leisurely and erratic hours. Edward was a good sport about the jab at him. The next question was directed to one of the popular young British bachelors, Tony Skyrme, just arrived and knowing nothing about our intricate maid-service system. "If a theoretical physicist's wife is pregnant and expects twins, although Doc Nolan isn't quite sure, and the father certainly hopes not, and she already has one small child and a three-eighths job at Tech as a technician that she will quit on labor day, the question is: How many half-days in Indian maid service is she entitled to?"

The bachelor stood up to answer, and when the laughter died down, he said, "Does the factor of whether the father is a good theoretical physicist enter into the calculations ?" This was regarded as a sufficient reply and the bright young man was applauded again.

Every group gave a party at one time or another, and they were all successful. It was hard to fail, as everyone came with high spirits every time. We were going strong on parties when my friends, the Allisons, came up to live. Sam had been kept in Chicago, coming frequently as a VIP. I knew our hectic and organized life would be frowned upon by Helen Allison, for I had kept her posted on details of our Mesa life. She had written me that we would all crack up if we didn't slow down, especially on social life. But we, on our high-altitude Mesa, thought we could live it up forever, and the mere thought of returning to a sane and prosaic civilian life sounded flat and dull. We were having the time of our lives, or so it seemed at the time.

I went to the East Gate to meet the Allisons, to see how she and the children reacted to their first view of the town. Helen, unlike some of the rest of us, liked to try to look sensible. She wore her hair straight, scorned frills and tried at that time to appear more reasonable than the rest of us. As she looked over the installations and factory-type buildings, with lots of people rushing around in old sloppy clothes, her first remark was, "It's far, far worse than you wrote me." Later she held firmly to the opinion that everything was more ugly and messy than necessary, and that the Army should have been more firmly overridden on the plan of the residential area.

Our social activity continued at a high pace until the last of 1945. The general atmosphere on our Mesa was not one conducive to contemplation, although the country around us had always been suit able for contemplative pursuits. Helen and others were quite right in finding something incongruous about all our "souped-up" social activity when we could have had quiet and maybe more rewarding weekends. Even on our trips to Santa Fe we were largely concerned with buying up supplies for parties, instead of using the days in that old city just to walk around and soak up the historic charm. But there was a world war on, and we lived and focused our lives on an Army post.

By the time our last June came around, a joint party was given by the Brodes, Allisons and Tellers in the Lodge. The Mess Hall roasted a large piece of beef—ration-point free—and sold us a whole round of cheese. Mici and I made cookies and pastries for days, and the afternoon of the party we took carloads of food and platters to the Lodge and set them out in the small dining room that could be locked. When we opened the doors to the food at about 11:00, it looked plentiful and appetizing. The next time we three hostesses saw the table, every scrap of food had been devoured by our hungry guests, since meat and cheese were rationed and a great treat. But the three of us didn't get a bite, not one, although, fortunately, the men in our families did.

Moll Flanders wrote a special ballet for the party and advertised the show: "Moll Flanders Ballet Company presents the premier of an original ballet 'Sacre du Mesa'." Everyone in the ballet had training, except Moll himself, who impersonated General Groves. But as Moll pointed out, although he had no ballet training, probably neither had the General. Ellen Weisskopf had danced in Denmark before her marriage, and Elsie Tuck had danced in England. Keith Allison appeared as Oppie and danced on a large table, wearing a pork-pie hat and semi-Army clothes. The main stage prop was a mechanical brain with flashing lights and noisy bangs and sputters, which did consistently wrong calculations, for example, $2 + 2 = 5$. In the grand but hectic finale, the wrong calculations were revealed as the real sacred mystery of the Mesa. Music was a record of one of Gershwin's concertos, which lent a futuristic tone to the production. The ballet had a prologue and epilogue: a workman halfheartedly sweeping across the stage holding a Coke bottle in one hand, before and after, exactly the same to him. The show was hilariously received by the one hundred or so guests, and some of the Washington VIPs who heard about it hoped we would put it on again. But the premier performance was the last.

The rest of the show consisted of torch songs by Kay Anderson, a cakewalk by Mary Argo dressed in garish costume with her face blackened, accompanied by Willie and his accordion, and a demonstration of two square dances.

Not all parties were large and hilarious. There were many small and quiet dinners, with serious and tense talk. Probably our most illustrious VIP was the generally beloved Danish physicist Niels Bohr, who was officially known as Nicholas Baker but affectionately known on our Hill as "Uncle Nick." His dramatic escape from

Europe in a fishing boat under the noses of the Nazis and his trip to America in a high-altitude bomber were among the top secrets of the war. He came often to Los Alamos with his son Aage, who was also a physicist, and the two could often be seen slowly walking around the Mesa, going to visit some of their many friends. One evening, after dinner at Elfreda Segré's, we sat very still and listened to Uncle Nick tell of his experiences outwitting the Germans. His voice was so low-pitched and his accent further complicated by constant lighting of his pipe that we had to strain to hear. He used up an entire box of large kitchen matches as their burnt ends piled up in an Indian pottery ashtray on the table.

Strange as it may seem, despite our well-deserved reputation as a marriage bureau, I do not remember any large wedding parties on the Mesa. Most weddings were very quiet and held elsewhere. Several ceremonies were performed at the Santa Fe home of Dorothy McKibbin in the early days of the project. Dorothy's house, with its carved Spanish doors, antique furniture, and windows overlooking the lights of the city, was a romantic setting for a wedding. The first to wed there was Priscilla Greene, Oppenheimer's secretary, who married a young physicist, Robert Duffield. Another wedding was that of Marge and Hugh Bradner, also a secretary and a young physicist. The ceremony inside was the usual, but outside the house our MPs kept close watch, for not only was Oppenheimer the "father" who gave the bride away, but one of the guests was Deak Parsons, and both men were under constant guard when off the Mesa. It was as secure a wedding as any bride could wish, although Marge was rather startled when she first noticed the MPs standing with guns in the open garden. Marge was never able to write of this to her parents, who also did not know the last name of the bridegroom until Marge could be addressed as Mrs. Bradner.

When V-E day came, it was duly announced over the loud-speaker system in Tech, but no special town celebration was planned. The men were working on special jobs for a testing deadline and many of them were off the Mesa. Each neighborhood hastily tried to think up some way to celebrate, but no one appeared genuinely enthusiastic. Perhaps we were getting tired at last.

In our neighborhood Erica Staub started things going by inviting

Bernice Brode (left) chats with her Tech Area boss, Donald "Moll" Flanders; his wife, Sally; and the R. D. Richtmayers at one of the many Mesa parties.

everybody to come to her house and bring a bottle for celebration. But it was not a lively gathering so when the bachelors from the Big House came in search of "Mesa widows" for dancing, we walked over there. It was not much livelier there, either. I remember Otto Frisch sitting in a corner making caricatures of all of us as we tried to dance. I also remember waltzing with Klaus Fuchs, who was an excellent dancer. Our conversation was lost in the outburst of a drum beat as Dick Feynman, one of our colorful characters, dashed about trying to arouse us into action. He called us all stuffed shirts and made us join a serpentine and wind around the Mesa shouting to wake everyone up. A few more joined us, and we ended up with Otto playing soft nostalgic Viennese music on my piano.

Bernice Brode enjoyed a dance with Jim Tuck, the first British male she encountered on the Mesa.

11 The British Mission

President Roosevelt and Prime Minister Churchill personally arranged for an American-British collaboration on the atomic bomb. Most of the work was to be done in the United States because Britain was under fire from German rockets. To head the British effort, Churchill chose Sir James Chadwick of Liverpool University.

So, in late fall of 1943 members of the British Mission began to arrive. The first to arrive were Otto Frisch, nephew of the Swedish physicist Lise Meitner, and Ernie Titterton with his wife, Peg. Otto was housed in the Big House with the senior bachelors, and the Tittertons occupied one of the tiny log houses beside the Lodge. Before long about twenty Britishers arrived, including Bill Penny, Tony Skyrme, Greg Marley and several others, mostly without families. All were put in the Big House and ate meals in the Lodge instead of in the Mess Hall, like our young dorm-living bachelors. The families came later—the Chadwicks, Moons, Tucks, Bretschers and Peierls. The last year two Canadian families came up—the Placzeks and the Marks—who were considered a part of the British Mission.

Most of the British Missionaries came to Los Alamos without seeing any other part of the country except perhaps for a day in New York and a change of trains in Chicago. This was a rather abrupt introduction to the U.S.A. They had to adjust to an altitude of more than 7,000 feet, a dry climate with hot midday sun and a most un-British way of life, including the strange aberration of their native speech. They were good sports about everything, which they accepted at face value. I was never sure, even after they had lived with us for two years, that they could distinguish between what was typical of American life and what were only the vagaries of life at Los Alamos. Although I constantly assured them that home was never like this, I suspected they secretly persisted in believing that all Americans loved overheated houses, ice cold food directly from "fridges," a happy-go-lucky community life with a minimum of privacy, no individual hedges to trim, and hectic days of long work hours designed to meet a deadline. On the whole, hadn't life at Los Alamos rather confirmed the accepted British picture of America? Here were a pioneer people starting a new town, a self-contained town with no outside contacts, isolated in vast stretches of desert, and surrounded by Indians.

Peg Titterton was the first British wife to appear on the Mesa. We made her acquaintance at once, inviting her to tea in the neighborhood. The first British male subject I encountered was Jim Tuck, when he came to a Saturday square dance, knowing nothing of square dancing, of course. "What exactly is square about it—the people, the room, or the music?" he asked as he took his pipe out of his mouth. He was very tall, with big blue eyes and a bland look on his face. He wore a shabby tweed jacket, flannel "bags" and always red morocco leather slippers on his tremendous feet. When asked why he wore the red slippers, he invariably replied, "Why, bless you, they are the only color slippers I've got." He wore them everywhere and when they wore out, he got some Indian beaded moccasins in Santa Fe. He lived at the Big House where Montoya, the picturesque Indian janitor, liked to talk with his charges. Once Jim said to Montoya, "I'm indeed delighted to find that the American Indian is not a vanished race," whereupon the Indian smiled his inscrutable smile and asked Jim about an engineering problem he was pondering.

Jim was from Oxford and fulfilled our idea of what a Britisher would be like. We loved to hear him talk, and people asked him questions just to hear his amusing accent. A well-wisher inquired how he was, by way of greeting, and Jim looked at the young man with a surprised gaze, "Why fit as a fiddle, why do you ahsk?" Jim complained about not getting his wife over from England. "I shall blow up this place proper, you know, if my little wife doesn't get ovah heah. She's a tiny little one, no bigger than a minute, won't take up much war space."

His wife, Elsie, finally got passage over and proved very useful in the community. She was a ballet dancer, and helped in school theatricals and private shows, and conducted a class for a few children who qualified. The Tucks had an apartment on the West

Road and bought an old car for Sunday trips. Jim had no interest in local ruins, claiming he had seen plenty of fresh ruins in England before he came over. His idea of Sunday trips was to try to shoot a bear, and although he never got one, his near-misses made amusing dinner-party stories.

The Egon Bretschers, with their three children, were housed in the apartment below us. The only other British family with children was that of Rudy Peierls, who took over as head of the Mission when the Chadwicks were not stationed on the Hill. Genia Peierls was a popular, forthright character.

None of the British wives could take paying jobs on their visas, so they entered into affairs of "Mesa business" instead. Genia was activity itself and most impatient with any lack of enterprise. She was born to come to the rescue if plans got bogged down. Our first experience with her ability was during a PTA meeting at the school, when we were discussing ways and means of recouping our loan library. The nucleus of this library was the books we inherited from the Ranch School, plus new ones a committee had collected money for and bought. It was kept in the living room of the Big House until absolutely all the books had disappeared—borrowed and never returned. Requests for returns were put in the *Daily Bulletin* from time to time, but all in vain. So in this meeting, Genia arose and, with an air of finality, announced the solution to our problem: "Most simple, I fetch books for you, one day only. Just give me a pram."

Her voice inspired confidence, so Honi Bretscher offered little Peter's pram. Next morning Genia marched from house to house demanding library books. If no one was at home she pushed the kitchen doors open and barged in searching for books from the library collection. These she put in the pram and took to the Big House, put them on the shelves and started out again for more. By nightfall she had covered the entire Mesa and the empty shelves were filled again. True, a number of people subsequently complained about loss of personal books, but on the whole, her forthright methods were greatly admired.

There was quite a community stir when the grapevine had it that the Chadwicks were coming to live on the site. James Chadwick and Sir Geoffrey Taylor visited as VIPs but did not live there. The Army went to work on a rather large log house in back of the small one fixed for the Tittertons, installing heat, remodeling and varnishing. We called it "glamorizing," and thought it one of the finest habitats on the Mesa when it was finished. But, alas, when the Chadwicks came, they clearly regarded it as downright primitive, and said as much. They did not stay very long, but moved to Washington. Before they left they gave themselves a party, inviting all their many friends.

At the end of the war, while the Chadwicks were in residence in Washington, Lady Chadwick authorized the British Mission at Los Alamos to give a farewell party for their friends on the Hill. She made out the guest list and ordered formal invitations printed on white cards, which were put into the mail cubbyholes in the Tech Area. The invitations were noteworthy as an abrupt change from the usual party invitations mimeographed on Army paper. We were summoned to a party celebrating "The Birth of the Atomic Era," to be held in Fuller Lodge. Everyone understood it was to be a special event and got out their best formal clothes, from mothballs if necessary, in preparation.

There were then six British wives, counting Else Placzek from Canada, with Genia in charge. They held council for weeks, usually in Honi Bretscher's apartment below us. All arrangements were "most secret indeed" (the official British equivalent of our top-secret category). Everything that is, except Genia's voice, which carried up to my rooms quite often. Many plans were afoot, that was plain, and in several ways my help was enlisted. Elsie Tuck asked me to take her to Albuquerque to purchase port wine. Port is the British ceremonial drink for toasts, and Lady Chadwick had ordered them to buy the best quality to be had in the region. The party involved several hundred people, so the bill for the port and for other wines and whisky and brandy was staggering. It was great fun to spend British Embassy money, which Elsie had in cash dollars in her purse.

On the way home Elsie began to discuss the problem of glasses, which was also her responsibility. She had about decided that paper cups were the only answer, a most un-British manner of drinking to His Majesty's health with the best port. There was no rental service in Santa Fe, so we thought we might see what could be had in Woolworth's. We went in and asked for the manager, who listened

Peg Bainbridge, Bob Brode, Helen Allison and Darol Froman paused for a chat during the dressy British "Birth of the Atomic Era" celebration.

with great interest to Elsie's tale, in her British accent, of the plight of His Majesty's Government of Great Britain officially entertaining in the American desert without any wine glasses for drinking toasts. He had nothing to offer but small unstemmed punch glasses, which he agreed to "loan" us. We deposited a nominal sum, and loaded my car with several hundred small glasses, all they had in his store. I told Elsie I thought Woolworth's ought to have one of the toasts, along with the King and the President.

Dinner was at 8:00, so on that warm September evening couples from all over the Mesa could be seen sedately walking toward the Lodge, dressed in full evening regalia. A few women even managed long gloves, never before seen in our town, and, some of the men wore white tie and tails. We were formally received on the open porch by one of the younger men acting as announcer in the British fashion, loudly calling out our names as we approached the formal reception line of the senior Missionaries. Then we were offered Scotch and soda or lemon squash. Dinner was formally announced in great style, and we went inside to find our places.

The grand finale of the British skit was the re-enactment of the Trinity test with a high tower (the ladder) from which a pail of stuff was overturned to make flashes, bangs and clatters.

The five or six British wives, assisted by a few of the young men, served the entire meal, which they had also cooked. We had thick soup prepared by Genia in pails the day before, and served, in the thick restaurant bowls from the Lodge. Next was a steak and kidney pie made by Peg Titterton, Else Placzek and Honi Bretscher and served on paper plates. For dessert there were individual paper cartons of trifle, which I had seen the day before at Winifred Moon's, on the window sills, in corners, stacked on the sink and even in the small bedroom. Winifred said later she never cared to see trifle again as long as she lived.

Notables such as the Peierls and Oppenheimers sat at a "high table" with Jim Tuck who acted as toastmaster. He rapped for silence and proceeded with the formal toasts, which we tried to follow with the right wines—we had three kinds—but some of us got confused. Port was reserved for the King, the President and the Grand Alliance.

Dancing to the usual collection of Mesa records followed the pantomime.

After dinner we all helped put up the tables and arrange the chairs to view an original skit in the British holiday tradition. It used "Babes in the Woods" as a basis. Good Uncle Winnie had sent his Babes to join forces with Good Uncle Franklin to outwit Bad Uncles Adolf and Benito. All that befell the children on their hazardous journey to the Unknown Desert was acted out by the entire Mission. Security was dealt within the first act, and Jim Tuck, who had written the skit, claimed he had cleared it with our real Security office. The security officer was dressed as the devil, with a long tail that had a red tail light at the end. The gate was rigged up as a mess of wire entanglement, and inside everyone had footprints taken, which were duly pinned on their backs for identification. There was a large safe, and when a document was taken out it had to be chewed up and swallowed. The next scene was supposed to be in a typical greenhouse apartment, dominated by an icebox into which the tenants retreated when overcome by the heat. The grand finale was a re-enactment of the Trinity test, with a high tower from which a pail of stuff was overturned making flashes and bangs and clatters for several minutes. This was not entirely comprehensible to many of the women, but made a tremendous hit with the men, particularly some of the details of the bangs. It was a smash hit.

After clearing away the chairs for dancing, we took formal leave of the hosts and hostesses, by that time pretty tired from their combined efforts as hosts, cooks, waiters, masters of ceremony, bartenders, actors and production managers, all accomplished in the special British manner in spite of difficulties. Surely it was one of the finer moments of the Grand Alliance.

12 Los Alamos and the Indians

Our contact with the Pueblo Indians of New Mexico began with the working relationship we had on the project. Army buses brought Indians from several pueblos up to the site every day except Sunday. Quite a number lived on the Hill and were given apartments on the same basis as the rest of us. The most picturesque Indian living on the Hill was Pop Chalee from Taos, who was married to an Anglo machinist. An artist of considerable reputation, she wore artistic clothes and long blue-black braids that reached below the waist. She had a job in one of the women's dorms, and several times gave lectures in Fuller Lodge on Indian customs.

Anita and Popovi Da, from San Ildefonso, had an apartment on the site until Po was taken into the Army. After he was sent back to the Hill, he had to live in barracks. Po was a technician in Tech, and Anita had partial charge of the Maid Service Office and later was housekeeper for one of the women's dorms. While they lived on the site, their son Tony, three or four years old, attended the nursery school. After the family gave up the apartment, Tony went to live with his grandmother, Maria Martinez, the potter.

I learned from my Indian friends that we Hill-folk were liked because of this working relationship. It was the first time they had known any group of "Anglos" who were not primarily interested in their welfare or curious about their cultural patterns. We accepted them as a part of our life on the Mesa. We began to visit their ceremonials and fiestas like any other tourists, but before long we went to the pueblos as their guests.

I first met Po at the Sadie Hawkins Day party, when our square dancers were waiting backstage to put on a demonstration. Po and was waiting, too, dressed in feathers and paint for his war-dance number, and looking very glamorous and wild. I had never seen an Indian dancer before, and he had never seen a square dancer, so we smiled shyly at each other. Later when we passed in the corridors at Tech, both of us dressed in drab work clothes, we recognized one

The world-famous potter, Maria Martinez, dances with the author's husband, Robert Brode.

Maria and her grandson have a friendly chat with Enrico Fermi.

another and always smiled. Once I asked why he didn't come to our Saturday dance group, and he promised be would. He did, with his pretty part-Spanish wife, Anita, and they learned to do the figures with very little help. Whenever they were on the site Saturdays, they came to our dance, wearing western-style clothes as we did.

On her way to the dorm where she worked, Anita often stopped to talk about Mesa affairs. Later on, when she started taking lunches at our house, we sat and gossiped about things in general. I learned a lot about the young Indians' thinking: how they want to remain in the pueblo but want a better life for their children than they had. The old people wanted to keep things as they were. Anita was saving money for a new house with an inside bathroom, good heating, and an icebox like the Army provided for us. Maria, on the other hand, was very strong-minded and resisted any improvements. Po wanted to fix up an electric kiln for his mother's pottery, but Maria would not hear of it. Once when I watched Maria and her sister, Clara, fish out the black pots and platters from the firing hole in her yard, about one in three pieces was badly chipped or broken—a terrific waste of her beautiful bowls, I thought.

Anita and I talked about how the Indians feel about their dual system of religions. They are all good Catholics and at the same time have their traditional gods and ceremonies. It seemed very strange to us to watch the corn dancers bring the Catholic saint from the church and place it in a shrine set up for the day, then perform the ancient dances that had no relation to Christianity. When the dancers stopped to rest, they had a choice of either going into the kiva, or kneeling in the shrine to pray before the saint. At sunset the dancers, still in corn-dance costume, carried the saint back to the church. But Anita saw nothing strange in this—they had always been so since the Spanish Conquistadors forcibly converted the conquered Indians.

The Indian dances, whatever else they meant to the Indians, provided good fun and a show for everyone. Los Alamos people provided an enthusiastic audience, and the Indians liked it. Some of the dances were held on weekdays, but when it was understood that our men could come only on Sunday, their one day off, some of the dances were switched. The dances also increased in variety, we noticed, and we suspected the Indians were making up new non-traditional ones, since we were enthusiastic but uncritical and would not know the difference. We heard tales from Santa Fe people who knew the Indians well, that the influence of Los Alamos was deplorable, that we actually encouraged the Indians to break away from tradition. Most of us felt that many Indians were tired of being pressured to remain so traditional for the benefit of tourists and even their well-wishers.

Some of the young men from the Hill wired San Ildefonso for electricity, and soon refrigerators and appliances made their appearance in the pueblo. Such improvements were not artistic or romantic, but they made life easier. We were rather shocked ourselves to find Grand Rapids furniture, brass bedsteads, linoleum floors, soda pop, and ordinary dishes in Indian houses. Some of us had more Indian crafts in our Army apartments than the Indians had in their houses. I set my table with Maria's black plates and candlesticks, while Maria herself set the table with a store tablecloth and store dishes. I once saw on a corner bureau in her front room a new set of pink pottery mugs and pitcher, of the kind bought in any ordinary store, with a card tied on saying "Happy Birthday to Maria." I looked across the room to her display of black and terra cotta pottery for sale, laid out on lavender oilcloth, and wondered how this could be.

Maria loved her pottery even if she did not eat from it. In our last year, Margery Crouch arranged with Maria to come up to our school with all her pottery-making materials, including extra clay for the children. She squatted on the floor at the school and demonstrated each step of the process. She didn't say a word—actually she spoke very little English—but held their attention for hours. Her quiet charm and dignity as she worked carried over to the children as no lecture could have done: She coiled her pots and smoothed them with small stones and her thumb. She gave each child some clay and took their work home to fire in her next batch. In due time, her son Po brought back the children's pots, all fired.

The first year we were timid about eating at pueblos on Feast Days. We thought one had to be especially invited to go into the houses and eat, which we saw everyone else doing. Soon we caught on that Feast Day is open house to anyone, and by that time we actually were especially invited by friends. The feast was always the same, dishes of stewed meat and pinto beans, with plenty of chile, two or three salads of pineapple, cabbage, apples, and raisins, Jell-O molds, canned peaches, spiced bread pudding, and a basket of pieces of bread from the round loaves baked in their beehive ovens, and plenty of butter and jams. The table was set with flowered oilcloth covering, then plates and forks and knives, and a cup without saucer for coffee. I used to wonder what they did with all the saucers, for they are usually sold as a unit. Each place had a bottle of soda pop—the cups were for coffee. Several times we brought along VIPs if any were on the Hill at the time, and they regarded eating in the adobe houses as a special bit of entertainment.

One of my half-days, Antonia Theresa from Tesuque, invited Helen Allison and me to come to her daughter's wedding at the pueblo. We accepted with interest, but had great difficulty finding out when it was to take place. Finally Theresa named the day and said, "Come early." So we went right after breakfast, hoping we hadn't missed the whole ceremony already.

The pueblo was deserted when we drove across the little wooden bridge and parked near some cottonwood trees. We walked around the plaza, looked into the church and found no one. We didn't know where Theresa lived, but I did know Ignacia, the governor's daughter who had worked for me, so we called on her. She, too, was vague about the wedding. In fact, it wasn't clear she even knew about it at all. So we went outside and wandered about the pueblo some more, watching daily chores such as fetching pails of water from the well and cooking some stew in a blackened enamel kettle on an open fire. There was no festive atmosphere as there was on dance days. Eventually we saw our Theresa come out of a house so we hastened over to speak to her and to give her the wedding presents we brought. She said. "You come to my house," so we went in after her to the front room where many Indians were sitting on straight chairs and some on the one double bed. We shook hands all around, as is the custom, although we were not introduced. Everyone sat quietly with no conversation. I was dying to ask if there was a wedding coming up, but I was afraid that would start Helen and me into giggles. We sat until around noon, when again Theresa came in and said, "You come eat now." So we followed some Indians into the next room where the table was set as it is for Feast Days. Theresa volunteered more information, "My daughter live Albuquerque, come soon," which she definitely did not do.

After eating we went outside again and discovered a small boy of about ten had been stationed on the bridge with a shotgun, which he said he would fire when the couple came over the bridge. So we waited until after 4 P.M. and still no wedding party. We found Theresa again and bid good-by, although she was plainly disappointed we were going. We were the only Anglos there and felt this was a very special chance we had of seeing a real Indian wedding. However, we had to get back to families on the Hill, and frankly we were awfully bored by this time. Later, Theresa told us her daughter was married in Albuquerque and came after 10:00 that night. The Indians danced all the rest of the night in celebration. We despaired of ever matching the Indian sense of time.

It was nice to go to a pueblo for a short time, and just sit and rest from a trip before going up the Hill. We loved the old cottonwood tree at San Ildefonso, with its wooden bench around the wide trunk, providing shade in the hot summer. The cottonwood tree was a convenient meeting place for relatives of ours whom Security allowed us to meet during the last year when they still could not come into our town.

Martin and Suzanne Deutsch asked Helen and me to go to San Ildefonso with them and meet his mother who would join us at the cottonwood tree. Helena Deutsch was an Austrian-born psychoanalyst who practiced in Boston, and Helen Allison was eager to meet her. On the other hand, Helena had never seen an American Indian, and Suzanne asked if I would introduce her mother-in-law to some. I was a little apprehensive because I found Helena very curious and prepared to ask many probing questions, which I knew the Indians hated and purposely do not answer truthfully. I have heard them tell dreadful whoppers to questioners, just to appease. I think it's very naughty of the Indians and I have told them so. Anita obligingly came out with her new baby, Joyce, over whom Helena went into ecstasies, of course. Joyce was a little brown doll with straight black hair sticking out in all directions and disappointingly clothed in baby finery from the best stores of Santa Fe. Anita was a good sport about the questions, which went like this: "Do you enjoy nursing your baby?" She giggled but was at a loss what to answer. She looked to me for help, but what could I do? Finally Po came out to join us, strolling over when he saw a distinguished lady who was sure to admire him. He could be quite a show-off and that day he pulled out all the stops. Helena said at once, as she clapped her hands, "I love him. He is beautiful," so Po offered to show her over the pueblo.

The grand finale of our association with the Indians took place on a cold December night of 1945 when the square-dance group from the Hill was invited to a party at San Ildefonso. It was a joint affair arranged in detail by Po and a committee from our dance organization. It was Po's brainchild, to celebrate the Atomic Age in general and the new relationship with their Anglo scientific friends in particular. Our committee went down to the pueblo one afternoon to look at an old recreation hall built by the Indian Service but long in disuse. It was big and bare and very dreary, but Po insisted it could be fixed up, the roof mended, decorated, and a stove put in. We then conferred with Maria, who apparently keeps close tab on pueblo affairs. She was against liquor of any sort, even beer, and took me aside to make me promise that none of our people would bring down any liquor. I promised on my honor, knowing how difficult this might prove to accomplish with some of my party-loving colleagues. I went the rounds personally to impress on any doubters that Maria said the party would be spoiled if any of us arrived with liquor, inside or out. This did not add to my popularity, and I felt like everyone's grandmother and a kill-joy. We bought several cases of Cokes, so dear to the hearts of Indians, and Anita provided fruit punch and pitchers of water to quench our thirst.

The day of the party arrived, cold and bitter, and a caravan of cars full of excited dancers rode into the pueblo past Maria's house with the blue door and parked by the hall. There was no electricity in the hall so our electronic experts brought along a special battery arrangement to run our record player. Po heard our cars and came to the door to take us into the hall. What a transformation! The walls were hung with evergreen boughs and beautiful Navajo rugs (I had never seen them before in anyone's home in San Ildefonso), kerosene lamps hung on the wall giving soft light, and a blazing fire burned in an enormous black stove. All the Indians were there, lining the huge room, holding their babies and looking after very old people. Most of them were dressed in fiesta clothes and for once looked like the colored picture books on Indians of the Southwest. There were about seventy of us. We allowed only our dance group members to come, with a few exceptions—Dorothy McKibbin, Edith Warner, Lois Bradbury, Helen Allison and Mary Mack—who were not supposed to tell they came. There was an air of festivity, and although we were shy at first, Po, Anita and Maria did their best to make us feel welcome. Maria was resplendent in satin and lace, jewelry, and white doeskin boots wrapped around her legs, smiling at everyone. Our men proceeded to set up our record machine, with a circle of Indian children watching with great interest. It didn't work too well, so after a while we fell back on ihe Indian drums.

Po made a speech of welcome, first in English, then in their native Tewa tongue. Whether he made the same speech in both languages, I have no way of knowing. There may not be a word for atomic nor for scientist in Tewa. The British Missionaries in our group whispered that Po exactly resembled an English county squire opening a bazaar. He certainly had the air of lord of the manor. He had been, too. He had made both sides of the pueblo unite for the party and work hard to get the hall and the food ready.

Some Indians opened festivities with a Comanche war dance, accompanied by the drums and a chanting chorus of men led by Montoya, our janitor from the Big House. Next Po called on us to put on a demonstration of square dances. We formed four squares, which we had practiced especially, with four callers—George Hillhouse, Matt Sands, Bill Elmore and an SED boy—taking turns. We used our most experienced dancers to give a smooth performance and make the best impression. Most Indians had never seen square dancing before, but after we finished we asked Po to invite everyone to join in with us. We mixed the formations so that some Indians were in every square, along with our experts. They are natural dancers. By this time initial shyness had disappeared. We all were laughing and having fun, but thirsty and out of breath. Cokes were opened and pitchers of water appeared.

The Indians opened the festivities with a Comanche war dance.

After this short interval, some of the Indian men, Cokes in hand, began to shuffle to the drums that had started up. They tied the blankets, which had been over their shoulders, around their waists and took hold of some of us, indicating we should shuffle around with them. Po shouted in Tewa the directions, which we gathered were for a sort of serpentine style dance game. The old governor led out, with his blue and white checked blanket tied tightly, his bobbed hair dancing, and his grin showing two front teeth missing. His moccasined feet kept perfect time, and he made gyrations with his arms that we were supposed to follow, sometimes one arm on the shoulder of the one in front, the other arm waving, or both hands on the head making like antlers. He also changed steps, which were rather intricate and sophisticated. We had to follow as best we could. Every so often we broke the serpentine line to dance with a partner. We formed circles and did any number of very fast movements, and, believe me, we had to keep our wits about us. The drummers went faster and faster. It seemed to be an endurance test so none of us dared give out. At the height of this excitement, with yells and shouts, Montoya got up on a chair and shouted above the din, "This is the Atomic Age—this is the Atomic Age!"

When the drums ceased , we flopped into the nearest chairs or on the floor to recover. Our row of friends sitting on the side lines clapped, and Helen whispered to me, "You have met your match tonight. These Indians can out-dance even you."

There was an intermission for eating. A long table, was set out with plates of food all looking unreal and exotic, nothing we had encountered before at Indian feasts. The pueblo wives, under prodding from Po, had dug up ancient recipes and produced almost forgotten pastries—prune pies like pemmican cakes. There were tiny tamales, tiny chicken rolls, tortillas, hot baked dishes with lots of chile, fancy squash mixtures, and the pieces of round loaves of white bread with butter and many kinds of preserves. There were strange things we could never figure out, but all delicious, and our hosts seemed to be enjoying the food as much as we were. There were pitchers of fruit juice and plenty of coffee.

The guests from the Hill were invited to eat first. I noticed the Indians held back, so I told Po that we wanted no segregation. He then gave orders in Tewa, and everyone joined in, took plates and helped themselves. Anita and other gaily dressed women stood in back of the table ready to help or explain. It was very graciously managed. We were full of admiration and many of us begged for recipes. As we were all eating and giggling, I noticed all the inscrutable expressions disappeared and every face was happy and full of excitement.

It was a wonderful evening, but by 2 A.M. we were tired out and thought we should not wear out our welcome. Besides, there was the long drive home. Anita and Po seemed to feel something was wrong that we could not stay longer, and they danced on and on. Po had wanted to invite *Life* magazine's popular feature, "Life goes to a party," so I wrote to the magazine asking if they would be interested in a party between atomic scientists and Indians, but *Life* declined. I think the magazine missed the boat. It was a first event of its kind.

No one planned any deliberate association of scientists and the Indians, but undoubtedly life at Los Alamos had its effect on the pueblos. When I revisited the pueblos in 1948, they were working for wages on the Hill and buying food in stores. They had new pieces of furniture, new appliances, and the Spanish houses near Española had new wings and porches added and, in general, looked more prosperous. In the pueblos there were a few inside bathrooms,

A table was set out with exotic looking food unlike anything the guests had encountered before at Indian feasts.

and some brand new adobe houses. Maybe their contact with Los Alamos had less to do with this than the fact that they earned money now. Their economy was now tied to Los Alamos. New AEC buses replaced he Army buses and fetched up the Indians every week day. What effect this permanent association will have on pueblo life, I leave to the anthropologists to study. One result is clear: the Indians, like all the rest of us, have to think and worry about the new atomic age. This, in itself, tends to broaden life in the small pueblo world.

Several years later I visited San Ildefonso Pueblo homes of my friends of the war days. Nearly every house had cut out the current cover of *Life* magazine, a picture of J. Robert Oppenheimer with his porkpie hat, and tacked it up beside the sacred symbols on the walls. He looked just as he did when he came to their dances in the war years.

Edith Warner in her adobe home by the Rio Grande

13 Miss Edith Warner

The only friend we were allowed to visit who was not connected directly with the project was Edith Warner, a friend of Robert Oppenheimer. She lived in an adobe house by the Rio Grande, on land that was part of the Indian reservation of San Ildefonso. Her house, including two little guest houses in back of her own, had been built by the Indians, and she paid rent to Maria, the potter of San Ildefonso. Her house was about 20 miles down the winding road from our mesa. Oppenheimer arranged with her to serve dinners to people from the site. She called this her war work, as she only came out even on expenses.

Miss Warner, daughter of a Philadelphia clergyman, was a small, frail, very dignified lady who had settled in the Southwest many years before for reasons of health and to find a quiet peace where the hectic world could pass her by. She kept livestock, raised vegetables, and at one time was the station master of the Otowi Station on the Denver & Rio Grande Railroad, a narrow gauge system that went out of business just a few years before we came to Los Alamos. (A pity, as we could have put the railroad into the black in a few months.) Miss Warner was listed in the New Mexico Guide Series as a writer who has a tea room for tourists.

One day in the 1930s a young man came riding by on his horse, from his ranch in the Pecos Valley, and stopped for refreshment. He stayed all afternoon, and thus began a friendship that culminated in our dinners at Miss Warner's during the war, and which also, by an ironic twist of fate, brought the atomic bomb project to her very door. She became much concerned with the new atomic age and the direction it would take in the future. Before her death in 1951, she was given the newest treatments for cancer at the new Los Alamos hospital.

The same hand of fate that brought her to the Pajarito Plateau, seeking isolation from the mainstream of life, had also brought us to the same mesa country, also seeking isolation, but for a different purpose. That our paths crossed in the desert made our lives richer and hers more disturbed. Just after one crossed the old bridge on the Pojoaque road, there was her vine-covered log and adobe cottage in which she and Tilano lived. Tilano was presumed to be the oldest Indian in the region and known to be the wisest, but we never knew much about him or how he came to live with this prim lady from Philadelphia. Any secrets he had, or any he acquired from conversation of the world's atomic scientists, died with him two years after Miss Warner's death. They shared many secrets, pooled from two separate civilizations. It was one of the Oppenheimer miracles to have arranged for Miss Warner to serve dinners to us. For security purposes, her house was closed to any other tourists.

When we drove into the open space in front of her compound of houses and went into her kitchen,we found a different world from the one we had just left on the Hill. Her kitchen had a charm composed of Indian Southwest and culture from Philadelphia. Maria's black bowls sat on the open shelves with Miss Warner's family china. She cooked on a large black range, which she kept spotless and shining with her restless efficiency. I have always thought that Robert Oppenheimer remembered her lovely black stove when he and the Army gathered all the "Black Beauties" for our kitchens on the Hill, thinking they would lend the same gracious living to us. Alas, that concept was defeated in every way at Los Alamos, and not even romantic museum stoves could retrieve it.

Miss Warner had no plumbing. Tilano fetched water from the well outside the kitchen, and they washed from a corner washstand as our grandparents did. The kitchen was always warm with odors of food. We would have been content to remain there all evening, but we were directed to the other two rooms, where tables were set. The ceilings were low, with hand-hewn vigas, and whitewashed adobe walls. In each room was a corner fireplace where Tilano built fires of piñon logs, upended in Indian fashion, for more radiant heat. In winter, we huddled by the fires as soon as the meal was over, for there was no other heat. A long table, hand carved at the Indian School, was laid with hand-woven mats and Maria's black pottery plates, bowls and candlesticks. Except for the fire, candlelight was the only illumination. A soft light was cast on the old Indian pottery and baskets, and Indian paintings hung on the white walls. It was a scene of the Southwest from the picture books, much as many of us had hoped Los Alamos would look.

Miss Warner preferred only ten for dinner, but if a VIP suddenly came up to the site, she would stretch the reservations, particularly for her favorites, "Uncle Nick" Bohr and his son, Aage. The atmosphere was one of quiet talk. She frowned on any loud voices, and once scolded Jane Wilson and Genia Peierls for talking too loudly about Mesa affairs when Bohr was also a guest.

She and Tilano served the food, he in a bright blouse and his long hair in braids, and she in her usual trim shirtmaker dress and Indian moccasins. Her grey hair was brushed into a neat coil at the nape of her neck, and she wore no cosmetics, although she was very pale. She absolutely forbade any liquor of any kind. She called us her "hungry scientists," a term well earned by the generous amount of her good food we consumed. Everything was home-grown, home-cooked, and tasted delicious. In the sweet-corn season, Tilano went into their garden in late afternoon, picked the ears and shucked them in the field. Miss Warner dropped them into the kettle of boiling water as she heard our cars coming into her yard. We ate five or six ears apiece, with her butter. There were red raspberries in the summer for dessert, other times her luscious chocolate cake. We never stayed long after dinner, for it did not seem the thing to do, and we had the long ride up to our town. As we left through the warm kitchen, Tilano would be drying the dishes as Miss Warner washed them in a dish pan on the kitchen table. We paid $2 per person, and she would not take anything extra. When we became better acquainted with her, we realized her profit was too low to buy the things she really needed for herself and Tilano.

She had no phone and neither did we, so it became the habit in our neighborhood to ask anyone going into Santa Fe to stop and give messages to Miss Warner about reservations for dinners. This gave us a chance to talk to her when she wasn't too busy. She was a good listener; we could sit in her kitchen and tell her our troubles and regale her with tales of goings-on in our town. She did not see how we stood the high life of constant activity and agreed with Helen Allison that we overdid everything. She understood what our evenings with her meant to us and how we loved the peaceful romance of her surroundings even more than the excellent food she served.

In summertime, we took turns fetching surplus vegetables from her garden to sell on the Hill, a scheme Kitty Oppenheimer started. The ladies on the Hill fought over this fresh produce, particularly over the raspberries. Sometimes Miss Warner let us come down and help Tilano pick fruit. She did not like him to climb trees as he was growing old, and even the oldest of us looked young and agile to her. As more people came up on the Hill, her reservations were so much in demand that we had to divide them. The second year she could not keep up so many days, so conflicts developed with the "regular days" of the pioneer residents—the Oppenheimers, Wilsons, Bethes, Macks, Tellers, Bachers, Ed McMillans and Robert Serbers among them. We were in the second wave of residents. Some of us tried to invite not each other but those who could get no reservations at all. In truth, not everybody really wanted a permanent day; some just pretended to be slighted and took the attitude that dinners at Miss Warner's were a matter of prestige only. Finally Miss Warner had to stop dinners altogether, except to have the Oppenheimer family when they wanted to come by themselves. She always appeared frail, and her immaculate standards kept her working too hard. She worked too hard for us, which we did not realize in time, and we urged her on.

We stood in awe of Miss Warner and were always a little intimidated at her house. Even our children put forth their best foot when they stepped inside her house. No young children were brought to her dinners, but we often had some with us en route to Santa Fe or on trips. Once she allowed a birthday party for my boys, and we took down four guests. Along with their rougher memories of life at Los Alamos, I wanted my boys to have a memory of another side of the Southwest.

Miss Warner had one of her white turkeys stuffed and roasted, which Tilano carried in with mock ceremony, asking, "Who carve, who carve?" Without waiting for an answer, he placed the bird in front of Jack, whose big eyes, serious but childish, and mop of yellow hair were in contrast with his grey flannel suit with white shirt and tie. But Jack, on his 13th birthday, rose to the occasion undaunted and accepted the task without a word, exactly copying his father's expert carving technique. Miss Warner was much impressed and Tilano's eyes twinkled as he stood holding the plates. Jack heaped them so high, I remonstrated, but Miss Warner shook her head—this was their party.

After the turkey was cleared, Tilano brought in chocolate birthday cake with candles—thirteen for Jack and fourteen for Bill. He held the cake aloft, saying, "No chocolate cake for boys, make boys sick," and returned to the kitchen with the cake. The boys did not know how to take this but sat tight, wide-eyed, and sure enough, Tilano came back with the lit-up cake. He set it in front of Bill this time, who neatly cut it into wedges. There also was ice cream, an unexpected treat.

After dinner I shooed them all outside for exercise while we chatted with Miss Warner. Soon one of the boys returned and breathlessly announced that Jack had fallen into the Rio Grande. My husband dashed out and brought in a dripping, crestfallen Jack, who howled that he was pushed into the river. He was a sorry sight and covered with mud, but I was chiefly worried about Miss Warner's kitchen and the mess on her scrubbed floor. There was nothing to do but peel off the soaked clothing. Jack's chagrin was not helped by Tilano's giggles and obvious enjoyment of the situation. Tilano wrapped one of his blankets around Jack, while the boys danced around chanting, "Heep big Indian Chief, him fall in river." This delighted Tilano even more, and he clapped his hands. My idea was to get my party up the hill as soon as possible, so Tilano tucked Jack, blanket and all, into our car and, still laughing, waved until we reached the main road. It was clear that he, at least was thoroughly enjoying the evening.

Our last year brought many changes to the Hill and, in turn, to Miss Warner and her design for living. A new road to Los Alamos was in the offing, passing over a new concrete bridge replacing the wooden one and right through her front yard. The rerouting of all heavy traffic via Española, adding about 10 miles to the trip from Santa Fe to Los Alamos, had been a loss, and it seemed cheaper to build a new road. So Miss Warner had to move, and she and the Indians chose another site on the far side of the new road, nearer their garden. By that time, Norris Bradbury had succeeded Robert Oppenheimer as director, and a good many of Miss Warner's friends had returned to their homes. Lois Bradbury looked after Miss Warner until her death, cultivating the garden, taking the washing home to Los Alamos, bringing supplies, running errands in Santa Fe, and so on. Lois said her trips to Miss Warner's replenished her soul against the continuing hectic life on the Hill.

The new adobe house for Edith Warner was built by Sunday volunteers from Los Alamos, while the Indians from San Ildefonso worked on it week days. When I visited the pueblo in 1948, I heard tales that the Indians took down the work done on Sunday by the scientists and rebuilt things on Mondays, but there is no proof of this. At any rate, the house was a pleasurable joint effort of people from the Hill and the Indians. Miss Warner was quite ailing by that time, but she managed to feed lunch to the families who came to work. I was not there when she moved, but she wrote that it was a pulling up of her roots from more than thirty years of quiet peace. I stayed overnight in her new house, which was clean and fresh, free from drafts, with a covered porch and an extra bedroom, but it lacked the special aura of romance of the old one. Something intangible was missing. I suggested she was one of the victims of the new atomic age, and Tilano nodded as he turned his head toward the Hill. "Cars go up, cars go down—everbody full of talk-talk." It was an alien influence imposing itself on his final years of life, but he was too wise to try to find a solution. I suspected he enjoyed the added excitement in spite of his complaints.

But Edith Warner, Lois Bradbury, and I did try to figure things out, and we sat discussing the changes that had come over the quiet Rio Grande Valley and the Pajarito Plateau since the year 1943. Every Christmas, Miss Warner wrote a long letter for her friends, telling of the changes, in years and seasons. She and Tilano still recorded the date when the aspens first turned golden; Tilano still trained the dancers at San Ildefonso; they still raised ten varieties of squash in the garden; they still followed the daily routine of farm chores; but their spirits were not at peace. The disturbing new atomic age was developing on the Hill only 14 miles away now by the new road. The streams of cars reminded them daily that the world had an uneasy peace, at best.

The night I slept in Edith's own bed (she insisted she take the couch in the kitchen) and looked over the new room with white-washed walls, I saw the large photo of her friend, Robert Oppenheimer, in a frame on her Philadelphia dresser. He was the symbol of the scientists she came to love when they came to work in the desert—her desert. It reminded her that she had witnessed the revolutionary change in the scientific world, from an era of relatively small-scale university or industrial research to one of secret government multibillion-dollar projects.

All during our stay on the Hill in the war years, Miss Warner could not be induced to visit our town, saying it was better that she only hear about it and not see it with her own eyes. She would have loved our concerts, and we could have obtained a pass for her, I'm sure, but she said she belonged to her house, to her garden and to her valley. While she had much to give us, we really had nothing to offer her. In August 1945, she shared our jubilant success and our belief that the atomic bomb had shortened the war and saved lives— American and Japanese. Like us, she thought the bomb need never be used again, now that its devastation was known to the world, and that it might play a role in ending wars for all time.

On our last Christmas Eve, Helen and I persuaded Miss Warner to let us come and fetch her for her first visit to the site since the old Ranch School days, while we were still there. We promised to tell no one and have only a family supper. Tilano would not come at all. That night there was a blinding blizzard, and as we took her through the town past the water tower to our neighborhood, the dark storm softened the harsh slums and installations. Tilano had collected a pile of traditional piñon knots for her, and we built the tiny fire out in the new-fallen snow in front of our house. It is an old Indian custom on Christmas Eve. It was our first snow that year, and we put scarves over our heads as we watched the fire burn out, leaving the dying embers to make an earthen circle in the snow. Alice Smith and little Annie came out to watch with us, and we all had tears in our eyes as we watched the fire die. It was a closing ceremonial to our war years and to the intimate friendship we had made.

After Miss Warner died, Adam, son of Maria, and his wife Santana came to live in Miss Warner's house to look after Tilano. The spotless Philadelphia routine gave way to more casual attention to house and garden. The little valley near the Rio Grande was never the same again, because no one could follow in the footsteps of the meticulous, gentle lady from Philadelphia, with the artist's love for every wild bloom and colored rock and changing tree in the desert of New Mexico.

14 ALAS: Scientists in Politics

W hen my boys and I arrived back at Los Alamos in August 1945, after our first vacation in three years, we encountered a new life on the Hill. Work on the project was just idling, Oppenheimer was in Washington most of the time, and a new director was in the process of taking over. He was Norris Bradbury, commander, USN, one of the so-called "professors in uniform," who had been living on the site all along. And a new line of activity was going full tilt. Scientists had gone into politics, and the Mesa was buzzing.

I got immediate briefings from Alice, Jean, Helen and Mici, all talking excitedly at once. It seemed that rumors from Washington had reached the Hill that a bill for the continued military control of all atomic energy was being pushed through Congress without debate. This was a very serious turn of events for scientists, for all their futures would be affected by legislation for the control of atomic energy. More than any other groups in the country, nuclear scientists were in the unenviable position of knowing what this new energy was and what it could be. The frightening aspect was that the public, including congressmen, did not know. The general public was already getting false impressions, since every reporter worth his salt was getting into the act. This became evident from newspaper dispatches and commentators' columns all over the country. Sermons were being preached against the atomic bomb, resolutions were being passed to abolish atomic energy by all kinds of organizations, and the unfortunate idea was being created that atomic energy meant only destructive bombs.

To cope with this alarming national situation, the Association of Los Alamos Scientists (ALAS) was formed. A few of the younger men actually organized the new society, for the older, more experienced scientists either did not care or thought it hopeless to try and get atomic energy away from complete military control. Even Oppenheimer was in this category, along with most of the influential VIPs in Washington, although privately they all deemed it most unwise to place science under the military. So it was left to the young and uninfluential men to lead the way, and they did. Similar organizations sprang up at other government war projects, and soon they all combined into a national Federation of American Scientists. Membership was enlarged to include engineers as well as scientists, and some administrators.

The first president of ALAS was Willie Higinbotham of square dance fame and the life of our parties on the Hill. He now turned his enthusiasm and energy to the new organization and had no more time for parties. Our wartime routine had collapsed in any case, so many of us entered into the new activities with the zest of change. The women were tremendously interested in ALAS, and did not share in the rather defeatist attitude of our husbands that nothing could be done in Congress. We were not afraid of national politics. It was something we could understand, even if we did not understand science. Willie called a meeting at the school to form a women's auxiliary and outlined tasks we could perform for ALAS. The men needed office help and got many volunteers. Every morning Babette Chamberlain took dictation and typed. Others came, too, and were given errands to run. I offered to run a clipping bureau since there was no money at first to subscribe to one.

The men obtained an inner storeroom in the Tech Area for an office. It had no windows and no furniture, but some GI desks, along with a few chairs and a filing case, were moved in, and a blackboard and bulletin board put up. I advertised in the *Daily Bulletin* for newspapers to be brought to this little office, and each day I had a pile to take home. Someone on the site subscribed to every important newspaper in the country, and after a little coaxing brought them regularly. In my apartment my committee of neighborhood women sorted them and cut out any article about matters atomic. I took the clippings back to the ALAS office and filed them under headings the men suggested. When the hearings started in Congress, I posted reports on them so everyone could follow progress from our bulletin board.

The men were busy answering articles that gave false information, half-truths, or seemed to be propaganda for one cause or another. Editors and publishers were sometimes reluctant to take the word of unknown scientists against their paid commentators, so the boys of ALAS got Fermi, Bethe, Bob Wilson and a few others who were beginning to become known to the country to sign dispatches. ALAS got a lot of calls for lectures, and many "hit the sawdust trail" as the men called their trips to give these free lectures. They usually had to pay their own expenses since ALAS had no treasury at that time. Magazine articles were harder to place, and of course no one thought of asking for pay. The men used to say they needed their own publication to get the facts to the public, so the seeds of the future *Bulletin of the Atomic Scientists* were sown.*

A lot of resolutions were drawn up and the men sent the women all over Tech to get signatures, particularly of senior scientists who were too busy to draw up resolutions but would sign them if they agreed with whatever was expressed. I remember delivering the mimeographed resolutions, then going back next day to get the signatures. Sometimes we could get our own licks in, when some were leery of getting "into politics," by reassuring them it was necessary and their duty. Most scientists just don't like to see their names in the papers, but if a garbled account of science raises their blood pressure enough, they will speak out.

The original bill presented to Congress on atomic energy, known as the May-Johnson bill, placed all atomic science under the War Department as it had been during the war. The military wanted to keep it that way in peacetime as well. To insure continuity in work at Los Alamos, Oak Ridge and other government projects, the bill was to be rushed through Congress. No adequate debate was planned. Only a few scientists were consulted, behind the scenes in secret. Some of the senior officials such as Oppenheimer and Deak Parsons, who were in Washington and knew the climate there, claimed it would be useless to buck the powerful support the bill had in Congress and out. Therefore, the supposedly older and wiser and more influential members of the scientific community did not take an

Founded Dec. 10, 1945, the Bulletin of the Atomic Scientists is still published.

aggressive lead in this serious matter. When this fact became painfully apparent, some of the younger men got into the act and launched one of the strangest lobbies ever to hit Washington.

Willie felt he had a mission to fulfill, so he and several others took a bus to the nation's capitol at their own expense. They had no money, no office, no staff, and they certainly had no political knowhow. They had only the backing of their unknown and penniless colleagues on the Hill—our Hill, that is, not Capitol Hill, which distinction was the first lesson they learned in Washington. Their first object was to stymie the progress of the military control bill, then get one of their own drawn up for civilian control. I was not there to see how they operated, but the tales that reached our office at Los Alamos made some of their most ardent admirers wonder whether Willie and friends were not going too far too fast. *Newsweek* had written, "one of the curious by-products of atom-splitting is a lobby unlike any Washington has ever seen." The boys were getting lots of attention in the press. They were called "Babes with an Atom" and being interviewed as humorous curiosities by professional reporters. For instance, when asked what bloc of votes he controlled, Willie laughed and told reporters no one in his town of Los Alamos could vote at all. So some of the boys wrote to Willie from our windowless office to the effect that maybe it would be best if he would learn something about lobbying. Willie promptly wrote back that he had no time to learn anything, he was too busy giving lectures on atomic energy to any group who would listen, especially Congressmen. "They want to learn all about atomic energy in ten easy lessons."

The boys also asked Willie how his money was holding out and he wrote, "I don't need any money. The people here are very generous and pay all the bills. They know we have no money. Don't worry, I'm eating better here than you are at the Mess Hall."

By all reports he had the Congressmen and newspapermen working so hard nights that he began to take along his Stomach Steinway and had them square dancing when they got tired of atoms. Willie later denied this, but those were the tales we heard on the Hill at the time. So we relaxed and thought maybe the Congressmen were getting their money's worth and having the time of their lives. We heard also that Robert Oppenheimer was giving lectures on atomic energy, with eager audiences crowding to hear. Willie and friends were also contacting all interested organizations and explaining the merits of civilian control of atomic energy.

Willie came back to the Hill to report progress. He and the other scientists from Chicago and Oak Ridge had the support of the senator from Connecticut, Brien McMahon, himself new to Washington. He had written and introduced a new bill for civilian control to replace the old May-Johnson draft. We called a mass meeting at the Lodge, which was jammed, to hear the reading of the first draft of the new bill. There were many "bugs" in the bill, which precipitated much argument. The Congressmen, as well as the military, seemed obsessed with "keeping the secrets" and did not believe that any other scientist except an American could discover anything. Even General Groves testified that the Russians, for example, could not make an atomic bomb before twenty years. In this first draft there was a clause that could be interpreted as providing the death penalty for inadvertently giving away any "secrets." This was eventually thrown out, but a lot of secrecy was kept in.

The chief gain of the McMahon bill was that it placed the government monopoly of atomic energy under civilian control, with a five-member Atomic Energy Commission appointed by the President and confirmed by the Senate. The bill also provided for a joint Congressional committee to be set up as a watchdog over the affairs of the AEC. Such a government monopoly, set up by law, was unprecedented in American history. The bill was passed after many amendments and was left intact until 1954 when it was amended to let private enterprise have a greater share in the development of atomic energy for peaceful purposes.

We had many discussions at our meetings about the possibilities of international control of atomic energy. Oppenheimer stayed in Washington as adviser to the President on this effort. The first matter of importance was to see that there was a clause in the national control bill that would allow for this later. The United Nations was set up that summer in San Francisco with a Commission on International Control of Atomic Energy. In those days it was a real possibility and not a mere dream. However, the idea got bogged down by wrong moves by the wrong people, in this country, in

Russia, and in the United Nations. But the seed of the idea was there and this was important. Public opinion was ahead of the statesmen for international control of atomic energy.

On our Hill, activities of ALAS increased all that fall. The men received constant invitations to give lectures, and the Army removed some restrictions on travel and visitors. An outgrowth of the Santa Fe Museum meeting, described in the next chapter, was the formation of a "Santa Fe Citizens' Committee for Atomic Energy," with the poet Witter Bynner as president. He wrote a barrage of poems to the new age and its scientists that were printed in the *New Mexican*. ALAS members were kept busy helping that city to organize mass meetings and discussion groups, to explain the McMahon bill and enlist their support. The Santa Fe committee raised money for ALAS, so at last the boys had cash on hand. They hired a part-time secretary, got a phone of their own, and had traveling expenses for more lecture engagements. I remember the excitement on the Hill one Sunday when Hans Bethe was to be on a national radio program, and we all stayed home to try and hear him on our radios in spite of the poor radio reception.

The delay in getting a bill through Congress did create uncertainty as to the future of Los Alamos, just as the military feared. The Great Exodus, as we called it, had begun in earnest and nearly every one faced a decision as to the future. Most of the senior scientists were on leave from universities for the duration, and always intended to return to them. But General Groves was genuinely hurt and alarmed when his "collection of crack pots" talked of leaving the site, where they had been happy to work for him the three war years. He misinterpreted this exodus as a revolt against the military once and for all.

As an example, there is the amusing experience of Sam Allison in Chicago in the early fall of 1945. One of the first private institutions to be reorganized to include research of nuclear energy was the University of Chicago. Sam, who had been asked to be director of the new Institute for Nuclear Studies, was invited to speak at a fund-raising affair in Chicago. There were lengthy ceremonies and poor Sam, who had a time clock in his stomach, did not get any lunch until so late that by the time he got up to speak he was mad. So he deviated from his written remarks with an off-the-cuff tirade that included cracks at the military and how they never would understand basic science research. For his part, he went on, he was so fed up with classified information that he was considering going into biology instead of physics to "study the color of butterfly wings for the rest of my life." Henceforth this was known as Sam's Butterfly Speech in scientific circles.

The War Department in Washington read about it in the papers and was so disturbed that General Groves dispatched two colonels to Chicago by plane next morning to interview Sam. They found him in his apartment in white duck pants and open shirt, prepared to play tennis before the Santa Fe Chief left for Los Alamos, where his family was living. He succeeded in assuring them that his speech was not the opening gun in an organized attempt to cast off the military, but blamed all the hullabaloo on his late lunch. Whereupon the colonels invited him to Sunday lunch before they flew back to Washington. They took him as he was— he didn't offer to change—to the swank downtown Hotel Stevens, where the hotel management declined to let Sam into the dining room without a coat and tie. He begged the smart looking colonels to take him to a lesser place, but by that time the hotel had fetched a coat and tie, which they kept on hand for just such emergencies, and Sam obligingly put them on. When Helen and I met him at Lamy two days later, Sam said the lunch was wonderful and well worth the tiff with the colonels and the hotel.

ALAS grew in membership and influence after its success in helping get the civilian control bill through Congress. The young men were taken seriously, and the older scientists ceased to be so wary of politics. Willie took a year off at his own expense and set up an office on K Street in Washington to direct activities in educating the public on matters atomic. ALAS eventually merged into the Federation of American Scientists.

15 Los Alamos and Santa Fe

No saga of wartime Los Alamos would be complete without including our relationship with Santa Fe, the long-suffering city that bore some of the brunt of our super-secret mushroom growth over on the Pajarito Plateau, 40 miles away.

With Santa Fe striving to retain its picturesque reputation and to resist expansion, it was not surprising that the caravans of shabby cars and large Army trucks mysteriously turning up the road to the Pojoaque Valley and to Española caused alarm among the citizens. In wartime no community can seriously object to Army posts being stationed in their vicinity nor take any overt action to obstruct them. The unusual secrecy precautions, including FBI and G-2 agents, the fact that no newcomers' names were known nor purposes of the new venture hinted at, and not even the exact location was revealed, not only annoyed Santa Fe but aroused grave suspicions. Anyone who ventured up the old Otowi road to see for himself where the caravans were heading was sternly turned back at the East Gate by armed MPs. All the new people gave one address—P.O. Box 1663, Santa Fe—to shopkeepers who asked for one. No accounts were opened in Santa Fe banks, and obviously none of us lived in Santa Fe at all.

As for us, we were told not to fraternize with anyone outside the project. Any necessary business dealings were to be strictly business. We were told that many agents were in the area to keep an eye on us for any breach of the rules. We took our secrecy indoctrination very seriously, no matter what fun we made of it. In fact, we cherished the hope that we would be taken for new artists and wealthy ranchers come to the region. But alas, we must have had our own earmarks to which not even our halo of mystery could lend glamour, for each of us was instantly spotted as "new people on the Hill" or "Site Y," as Los Alamos was locally called. I do not know how the people of Santa Fe knew our rules on security, or even if they did, but they made no effort to engage us in conversation or to meet us. We were politely disregarded in every way. In museums and stores we were treated as any tourist—or almost. As time went on, we realized it was known in the region where we were located, but our purpose was one of the best kept secrets of the war.

The influx of hundreds of new people into the area did cause hardships in such things as war shortages. The local people complained we were using up all laundry facilities, buying up parts for cars, hardware, and so forth. The shops and garages themselves prospered under our business as we were about the only tourists. The main worry seemed to be that we would change the atmosphere in the ancient sleepy town. We may have livened it up a bit with our brisk shopping tours and purposeful rushing around, but I doubt whether our presence affected the picturesque atmosphere well established in Santa Fe.

In these war years we often walked around the winding streets of Santa Fe, peering enviously over the walls into romantic and exotic gardens, adobe houses and chapels within. I remember Mary Shane had a relative living in a gorgeous set up, and she could not call on her. We walked by and took turns boosting each other up to see over the adobe wall. We saw cactus plants of great size and age, tropical buds, twisted trees covered with vines, old Indian pottery made into garden borders and a tiny chapel with an outside shrine. It looked all the sweeter for being forbidden fruit. Famous people we knew by reputation lived in the houses we walked by, but we despaired of ever meeting them. Perhaps they in turn despaired of ever having the mystery of Site Y solved in their lifetime.

Sooner than many expected, the news was out, and parts of the three-year jigsaw puzzle fell into place. Santa Fe buzzed with excitement and now-it-can-be-told satisfaction. That city had a right to feel they shared in the birth of the atomic era. When the Army secrecy ban was lifted in December 1945, we had a grand debut into Santa Fe society. It was staged by a special committee of Santa Fe citizens at the Museum of Anthropology, opposite Dorothy McKibbin's house. The museum was divested of its Indian exhibits and replaced with pictures of atomic experiments and Hiroshima damage. Enrico Fermi had a demonstration set up and explained it to groups gathered around. In the lecture room, a movie of Hiroshima was given two showings to capacity crowds. The main event was a program of speeches by several of our scientists, introduced by the Santa Fe committee. Vicky Weisskopf and Philip Morrison made the principal talks, standing on the stairs of the large hallway. Phil had just returned from Hiroshima and described the damage in graphic detail. Both men stressed the fact that the atomic bomb was made by representatives of many nationalities and pressed the hope that some form of international control would be the result.

After the lectures, a question period followed. Vicky called on a different scientist to answer each question, and each introduced himself and told where he came from before he answered the question. Sometimes the question could not be answered for reasons of secrecy or because no one yet knew the answer. The audience was most interested to see the "secret" people and to hear their opinions about the hopes and dangers of the new atomic age. Not one of us expressed a sense of guilt—quite the contrary, but many emphasized the dangers of uncontrolled use of such bombs for the future. A sense of realism marked all the answers; no harebrained idealism was evident that disregarded the facts of the world and its continued troubles and wars.

After this serious part of the evening, there was a social hour in the other museum rooms, with long tables set out with fine silver and china. It all looked very elegant to us, used to our primitive standards, and we stood around self-consciously at first. But it wasn't very long before the ice was broken. An elderly lady standing near me rapped her cane on the tiled floor and said, "Where are these scientists—I want to meet them. That's what I came for." So we introduced ourselves and from then on it was confused and bewildering with introductions and sudden invitations thrust upon us. Everyone invited us to have cocktails and tea, and it was impossible to keep dates straight in the general melee.

A confusion and profusion of social events followed in the next few weeks. At first we accepted with alacrity the many invitations that gave us the chance at last to see some of those romantic houses and to meet those renowned people—writers and artists and anthropologists. We wives were the most thrilled, but of course it was the men the citizens wanted to meet and talk to. We had difficulty with our men. After one or two parties, they balked—it took too much time out for the 80-mile round trip in cold weather. Our good husbands were not too good at being lionized; it embarrassed them, and they made no visible effort to improve. As a matter of fact, they gave out completely, long before we were satisfied.

But it was fun while it lasted, opening up a whole new world of old culture to our starved souls. It offered Spanish antiques instead of GI furniture, velvet drapes over paneled walls, old fireplaces with canopies on top where the Indian slaves slept in colonial days. Parts of ancient chapels were incorporated into rooms, and cultivated old ladies were present to converse with, instead of lively young people with their limited background. The parties were enchanting and the people stimulating and varied in types, although there was no time to know any of them well. The invitations were very impersonal—Mrs. X would send word to Dorothy McKibbin that she would like twenty scientists and their wives. Dorothy sent the invitation up to ALAS, where we posted a sheet on our office bulletin board with a "sign here" for Mrs. X's party. One of us was as good as the next, so everyone who wanted to could go to a party in Santa Fe.

Dorothy McKibbin introduced us to the painter Cady Wells, whose estate at Jacona in the Pojoaque Valley we had passed many times, always curious about the compound of houses and gardens on a bluff above the road. Inside, it was even more fascinating, a combination of New England and the Southwest, like Miss Warner's, only much more elegant. We had a lovely time, seeing his paintings and his collection of santos. After tea, we had a serious talk in which he said his beloved valley was now disturbed, with ominous sounds coming from our Hill, and no more could he paint. Years later I saw an exhibit of his paintings in San Francisco, and one of them was painted very dark, almost black, with a frightening smoke formation in the center. I remembered how he had told us that the shadow of our bomb had descended on his beloved valley and shattered his peace.

On our Hill, before the Water Crisis became acute, we had issued invitations to Santa Fe friends who had entertained us to come up to Los Alamos for a first tour of the town. They dropped all previous engagements and accepted the bid to see the mystery town. They had no idea of the difficulties our invitations involved, the first being to persuade the Army Security that such a venture was necessary or desirable. When permission was given, Dorothy McKibbin helped make out the list of guests and phoned them from her office at 109 East Palace. I believe the idea of the party was first generated by Rose Bethe and Jean Bacher, who organized committees to handle the many details. By this time the Bachers had moved into the log house vacated by the Chadwicks, and we had our planning meetings there—with a phone handy.

My job was to make out passes for each of the forty guests. It was necessary to get exact information for each guest, and after they were verified by Security, leave passes for them at the gate and notify each that some identification would be necessary. Dorothy instructed them all about this, but she phoned up to Jean that she feared some of them did not understand. Most of them were used to walking into places in the region where they were instantly recognized and had no idea that the Army might be different. A few days before the party, Dorothy phoned to inquire whether we had counted on several chauffeurs, as most of the guests did not drive. I timidly approached the Army again, who indeed had not counted on any civilian chauffeurs, nor would they. They were ready to call off the whole deal. "What is the place, lady, a country club?" they asked. "Who in h— wants to see this dump anyway?" So poor Dorothy, who was on our side, arranged car pools to get rid of the chauffeurs (who were dreadfully disappointed, it turned out).

Dorothy called two days before to warn us that we would be held accountable for the safety of the guests for 24 hours, the time limit of the passes. Awful thought, 24 hours. That possibility hadn't occurred to us. The guests were invited from 3:00 P.M. to the evening only. Surely all would go home. The whole affair had taken on an ominous flavor, and we began to be apprehensive.

The next day, the day before the scheduled affair, our water shortage became acute. No toilets flushed, and the taps were dry. So we decided to call off the party, even though we had all the food prepared and everything organized. We phoned from Jean's house and told Dorothy the party was called off. That evening we felt guilty and rather cowardly, especially when we heard from Dorothy. "Santa Fe is stricken," she said, not to see the mysterious city after looking forward to it. We were all cross and wrangled among ourselves. The experience of a water crisis can be most demoralizing, and we had been dealing with it for some time. Finally, after much consultation, we decided it would take our minds off our troubles to have the party after all. Some of the ladies would not go along with this change, but enough of us were in favor to carry out plans, so we called the sporting Dorothy again to say that the party was on and would she call them again? Dorothy was wonderful and never once accused us of being erratic, to say the least. With renewed energy and spirits, we proceeded with plans interrupted the day before. We even thought of cleaning up the roadside trash cans and ordering everyone to take in the laundries in view, generally hiding the flotsam and jetsam, but we reconsidered. We had endured all these features for three years; it would be false to pretty it up now. Our visitors might as well see things as they really were, in all the slovenliness. We were feeling sorry for ourselves, to tell the truth.

It was cloudy and cold, but no snow came to cover our water pipes. We had no time to worry about it, with last minute preparations in full swing. A piloting committee was ready to go to the East Gate at 3:00 P.M. to meet the guests and to see that the passes were honored. About 2:00 P.M., a girl came down to our house from the Lodge to tell us that the party had arrived and were being given tea, which we had arranged for as part of our plan—but at three, not two o'clock. We had to change plans hastily, for only part of them had arrived early. We started some on the tour of the town and waited for the remainder to arrive.

Our carefully made plans became more and more unworkable as the afternoon wore on. The tour was shortened when it got too cold, so some guests were sent to Mici's for cocktails where they removed their wraps and settled down for the evening. But our idea had been to go from one area to another, to see several houses, and to have the progressive courses we usually had. It was clearly going to be impossible to move our guests around according to plans. They were not mobile, so we decided to move the food instead. Mici took part of her Hungarian goulash to Helen and brought back salads. Elsie Tuck had far too much English pudding for dessert, but we didn't know who needed dessert at this point. Rose Bethe and Jane Wilson were coping with some guests up the road, and Genia Peierls and Laura Fermi had two carloads on the West road—or so we hoped. (They did, and wondered why we didn't come to change guests as planned.) As for our house, we did get our crowd up the front stairs to Alice's where tables were set, although we had more people than planned for. As things turned out, our guests were too bemused to eat at all, and they did not know who their hostesses were in any case. They had a good time in our house. All the husbands were on hand to talk to the ladies from Santa Fe, and we had two VIPs—Harry Smyth and Johnny von Neumann, as well. Apparently all the guests had been so appalled at our town that they were in a state of shock. One lady said to me, "I can't get over it, such nice people living in such a place all this time. Incredible, my dear, unbelievable, we had no idea." Around nine o'clock they talked of going home, so we faced the problem of getting them into their cars and getting their cars out of the mud and onto the right road to the gate. My husband had to get a jeep to pull one car onto the road. Finally, we checked on the guest list to see that no one was left.

My husband went down to the gate with them in our car to see that no one had lost a pass, which was needed for going out as well as for getting in. Finally, they were all gone, almost too hysterical to say good-bye. We were exhausted, too, but hungry, so we warmed up the goulash and all came to my apartment to finish up the food. As Johnny remarked, "That's what we have been missing up here— conversation with cultivated old ladies, just like the old days in Hungary."

Dorothy phoned a couple of days later and reported that the city of Santa Fe was now divided into two parts: those who had seen and those who had not seen.

The beloved water tower, with no icicles to sparkle in the winter sun, had failed the community, seeming to indicate that the work there was finished.

16 Water Crisis and The Great Exodus

While we were engaging in national politics on the Hill, going down to parties in Santa Fe, and thinking about going home, the Water Crisis was creeping up on us. The history of this crisis began in Washington when the project was being launched in early 1943. The cost of making the mesa site habitable appeared astronomical, so many facilities were set up as cheaply as possible on a gamble they would last out the war. The water supply was one of these gambles— a gamble on the weather, in this case. It was difficult and expensive enough to bring water down from the mountains to our water tower, an old one inherited from the former school, so the pipes were laid on the surface instead of being deeply buried in the ground as they should have been. It was hoped that a good blanket of early snow would keep the pipes from freezing, which it obligingly did the first two years. Our picturesque water tower, the symbolic center of our town, was filled to overflowing, with long icicles, which the children gathered when they melted and fell. But our third winter was cold and dry with almost no snow before Christmas. The annual ritual of the furnace stoking took place, and the sunny weather was welcomed for late picnics. We were unaware of the implications. We knew nothing of our precarious water supply.

When the Post authorities first began to worry about it, with more and more people coming up to live, it was kept top-secret. We later accused them of not worrying soon enough, but the major, when called on the carpet at a mass indignation meeting, produced summer *Bulletins* that contained notices warning persons not to water the victory gardens we had been encouraged to plant in the spring, unless we saved the bath water for that purpose. This latter caused much merriment, as the garden plots were a long distance from our houses. In any case we had no baths, only showers, as the Army knew full well. We had visions of dear "Ma" Hirschfelder, for example, carrying pails of dirty water to her plots of marigolds and daisies.

She brought bouquets to her friends saying, "I couldn't see raising onions and cabbages, don't you know."

It was not until October that serious notices began to appear in the *Daily Bulletin,* now stuffed in our mail cubicles instead of being delivered to our kitchen doors by soldiers in a jeep. Attention was called to the fact that our population was increasing and that "it would be advisable to limit the number of baths in each household to a minimum." The Army notices were always nicely literate.

By November every *Bulletin* carried some mention of water, suggesting methods of using water more than once, "after bathing the baby in the deep sink, save the water for the family wash, or "please use dishpans for washing dishes instead of running water." And, "it is recommended that floors be scrubbed with water previously used for washing vegetables," and so on. We followed the suggestions as best we could, but we did not worry unduly. For more than two years we had been wards of the Army and been well cared for, so we assumed no responsibility for our basic needs. We took the position that if we were short of water, it was up to the Army to get some more of it and stop fussing.

Bulletins began to carry boxed notices on water, for emphasis, and to include electricity shortages as well. We were admonished to become water-conscious and to conserve on electricity. We didn't have enough of anything. Soon tales began to come in from the West Road area, the highest on the mesa, that their faucets went dry at certain times of day. We discovered the authorities were turning off the water when the level was low in the water tower, and the West Road felt it first. Our faucets were the last to fail, for we were in the lowest area—"snob hollow" some called it. I invited young mothers to come and get pails of water from my taps, for babies' diapers (washing the vegetables first, of course). Finally our trickle stopped, too, and no toilets flushed. When anyone stopped by Miss Warner's, she sent up drinking water in jars from her well.

We remembered the bad fires we'd had in the summer, when the machinists' wing of T had burned down, sending up long licks of flame that could be seen in Santa Fe. That night everyone had left dinners on the table to rush over to the houses opposite the burning building. Hoses sprayed water on all the houses nearby from time to time before we could get away, and we were rather frightened. There had been other fires, too—the Owen Chamberlains' duplex house just up the road from our house had the roof burned off. When Babette Chamberlain came home from her job in T, the snow was falling right into her living room and covering the furniture. When Kay Manley's kitchen burned to a charred mess, all the neighbors pitched in to feed the Manleys while the Army rebuilt it. There was constant danger in the Tech Area from explosions, if fire should break out.

The water situation steadily worsened, with reserves never gaining, so the taps were turned off permanently. Frantic notices in the *Bulletin*, heavily lined with black, like death notices, told us to carry pails or anything else handy, up to the water tower, where the Army trucks would dispense water once a day. Each day a couple dozen trucks went down to the Rio Grande to fetch up barrels of water, and when they arrived back on the Hill, a siren would sound to let us know. From then on, the notices ordered instead of requested— boil all water to drink, come to the hospital for typhoid booster shots at once, and flush toilets at least once a day for safety. Only at this point did we learn that the pipes were frozen solid because they were laid on the bare ground in a country with months of freezing temperatures. Everyone was thoroughly incensed, including the doctors, who feared epidemics more than fires. We heard that Doc Barnett had phoned Washington, against orders, that he would not be held responsible for the public health if the situation were not improved at once. Our collective nerves were strained to the breaking point, and we vented relief at mass meetings at which Army officers were put on trial. Although it probably was not true, as rumor had it, that the Army was sending out battalions of soldiers with boxes of matches to thaw out the miles of frozen pipes, we quizzed the major mercilessly on actual methods. The major assured us that the pipes had been thawed out that very day, and we would have running water as soon as the reserves built up. When asked by a young housewife what assurance he could give that the pipes would not freeze again, the major turned purple with rage and snapped, "Madam, over my dead body will those pipes freeze up again." And he stalked out of the hall as it rocked with laughter.

At another meeting, Hans Staub slowly rose to his more than six-foot height and in his drawling tones read his calculated statistics of the estimated cost to the taxpayer of hauling water to the town. The officer gave Hans a cold stare while the audience clapped wildly. Of course General Groves got the worst of the blame, especially after folks heard reports of his remark when he heard the latest news of Los Alamos and the Water Crisis. Groves was reported to have said he didn't give a tinker's damn about those scientists, but he did not want the Technical Area to burn down. Our morale dropped to zero, or well below, even though the Army, by this time, was sending water trucks around the roads and stopping at each house to deliver water. Any receptacles set out would be filled for you by soldiers.

No other topic was heard in neighborhood discussions, only the water situation. One had to go over to the Tech Area to forget Mesa troubles. It was only natural that we suddenly began to talk of the homes we had left years ago—years and years, it seemed—and a wave of homesickness hit the Mesa. We dreamed of civilization, faucets full of gushing water, newspapers delivered to the door, milk set on the back steps every day, a school no one had to worry about, and a properly run community with a drugstore and no PX or soldiers' dance hall within earshot. Mici even waxed lyrical over street cars. "Paul would love a street car—never in his life has he seen one." All of us quarreled over the least little thing, and the only solution seemed to be to get out fast and to go home, if you had one. There was little incentive to remain. VPs went back to Washington with tales that Los Alamos was in a sorry state, rapidly disintegrating.

Our beloved water tower had failed us, indicating that our work in the desert was finished. The Great Exodus, which had been going on since August, now began in earnest. Moving vans could be seen on every road, blocking traffic. We had a rather gloomy Christmas, sitting on packing boxes in a house stripped of furniture. My Bill had packed up his room full of "parts" from the town's dump, and Army checkers had passed it all under Bill's watchful eye to see that they didn't delete anything. Our bicycles were crated, no parties were scheduled, and we had nothing to do except moan over the Water Crisis. We had been checked by the doctors and received certificates absolving the Army from any damages or something of the sort. Our family held council the Sunday before New Year's Day and decided to pack up our Ford and go home for New Year's, leaving the moving company to come for our goods. We went to see the acting commanding officer, Col. Stevens, and arranged for Bob to turn in our passes when he returned to finish his work. I could not face any farewells, so we just left as if for the day. Even Alice did not know at the time. I wrote everyone later. As we drove up our road for the last time, we passed the water tower. Mici and little Paul, both in red jackets, were standing gazing at the empty tower, with no icicles to glisten in the bright sun. We casually waved to them and drove on. A unique chapter in our lives had come to an end.

"Almost everyone knew that this job, if it were achieved, would be a part of history. This sense of excitement, of devotion and of patriotism in the end prevailed."

—From Oppenheimer's letter to the AEC, 1954

Glossary

AEC, the Atomic Energy Commission formed in 1946 for domestic control of atomic energy; functioned until 1975.

Army G-2, intelligence section of the Army's general staff.

Bandelier National Monument, a scenic park 10 miles south of Los Alamos featuring prehistoric Anasazi ruins.

Caldera, a large crater formed by the collapse of a volcanic cone. The Valle Grande is an example.

Duration, until the end of the war; as in, "We expect to be living here for the duration."

GI, nickname for enlisted personnel in U.S. armed forces; an abbreviation for "Government Issue."

Greenhouses, nickname for apartment houses in Los Alamos, always painted green by the Army.

Hectivity, coined by the author to describe the hectic activity on the Hill.

Kiva, an underground, or partly underground room, used by Pueblo Indian men for special ceremonies.

Luminaria, a sand-weighted paper bag in which a lighted candle glows; usually arranged in rows on roofs, walls and pathways as decoration for Christmas and other festive occasions. Also often called "farolito," meaning little lantern.

Manhattan District, a unit of the U.S. Army Corps of Engineers established in 1942 to administer the work of producing the atomic bomb; included major installations at Oak Ridge, TN, and Hanford, WA, and several others in addition to Los Alamos.

Maypole, pole decorated with streamers that May Day dancers hold while circling in and out around each other to create a woven pattern.

Otowi, the area where the road to Los Alamos crosses the Rio Grande. It translates as "the place where the river makes a noise."

Pajarito Plateau, the 7300-foot-high five-fingered mesa, extending eastward from the Jemez Mountains, on which Los Alamos is located.

Rationing, food rationing was initiated in January 1942. Ration books of stamps with varying point values were used for the purchase of meat, coffee, butter, cheese, sugar, canned fruits and vegetables and baby food, among other things. Gas rationing came later, with most drivers receiving "A" cards good for three gallons a week. "B" and "C" cards, permitting larger gas purchases, were issued to people in essential work.

Sadie Hawkins Day, a day, usually in November, when parties or dances are held to which girls escort boys; adapted from a race depicted in the "Li'l Abner" comic strip in which single women chased the bachelors.

SED, Special Engineer Detachment, a group of Army enlisted men selected for their special technical skills to serve with the Manhattan Project.

Site Y or Project Y, one of the Manhattan Project designations for Los Alamos.

Sopaipillas, a New Mexican pastry that puffs up like a pillow when deep-fried; honey is usually poured into its hollow center.

Trinity Test, the test in the desert near Alamogordo, NM, on July 15, 1945, of the first nuclear device that marked the birth of the atomic age.

V-E Day, May 8, 1945, the day the Germans surrendered to the Allies.

Valle Grande, one of the world's largest volcanic calderas, 15 miles from Los Alamos in the Jemez Mountains.

WAC, Women's Army Corps; its members are called Wacs.

Glossary of Names

Ed. Note: Gen. Leslie Groves is reputed to have described the scientists who gathered at Los Alamos as "the finest collection of crackpots the world has ever seen." Nevertheless, a remarkable number of the dedicated young scientists mentioned in this book were well on the road to significant achievement and some had already earned accolades for their accomplishments. Among them:

Bacher, Robert
Led the Weapons Physics Division at Los Alamos; hand-assembled the Trinity Test device at the test site; later served as professor of physics at Cornell University and chaired the Physical Science Division at Caltech. He was a member of the first Atomic Energy Commission.

Bainbridge, Kenneth
Headed the Trinity Test project in 1945 after leading groups dealing with instrumentation and high-explosive development at Los Alamos.

Bethe, Hans
German-born theoretical physicist fled Nazi Germany to U.S.; headed the Theoretical Division at Los Alamos; won the 1967 Nobel Prize for Physics for his contributions to nuclear theory and to understanding of stellar processes; headed presidential study of disarmament and helped negotiate 1963 partial test ban treaty.

Bohr, Aage
Physicist son of Niels, shared the Nobel Prize in 1975 for discovering the asymmetry of atomic nuclei; also earned the 1969 Atoms for Peace Award.

Bohr, Niels
Danish physicist credited with founding modem quantum theory; earned the 1922 Nobel Prize for Physics for investigation of atomic structure and radiation; began developing a theory of nuclear fission before escaping the Nazis to reach Britain by fishing boat and high-altitude bomber.

Chadwick, Sir James
Headed the British Mission at Los Alamos; known for the discovery of the neutron for which he received the 1935 Nobel Prize for physics; knighted in 1945.

Chamberlain, Owen
Physicist in Segré's radioactivity group at Los Alamos; later shared the
1959 Nobel Prize with Segré for discovery of the antiproton, a negatively
charged particle with the mass of a proton.

Fermi, Enrico
Italian-born physicist led the team that achieved the first self-sustaining
chain reaction in 1942 thus initiating the controlled release of nuclear
energy; awarded the Nobel Prize for Physics in 1938 for production of
artificial radioactivity by bombarding matter with neutrons.

Feynman, Richard
Theoretical physicist headed the Los Alamos group dealing with diffusion
problems; shared the 1965 Nobel Prize with Julian Schwinger and Si Itiro
Tomonago for contributions to electrodynamics; served on the presidential
commission to investigate the Challenger space shuttle disaster in 1986.

Fuchs, Klaus
Member of the British Mission and popular Los Alamos baby sitter, later
found to have supplied atomic secrets to the Russians.

McMillan, Edwin
Shared the 1951 Nobel Prize for Chemistry with Glenn Seaborg for work
on isolation of neptunium and plutonium; shared the 1963 Atoms for Peace
Prize with a Soviet physicist for discoveries that led to the invention of the
synchrotron.

Oppenheimer, J. Robert
Physicist renowned for leadership in developing a strong tradition of
theoretical physics in the United States, his outstanding direction of the Los
Alamos project and his prominent role as government advisor on military
weapons and policy in the postwar era.

Neumann, John von
Hungarian-born mathematician proposed an implosion method for making
nuclear explosion during atom-bomb development, pioneered in computer
science, and made important contributions to mathematics, logic,
quantum physics, meteorology and game theory; served on the Atomic
Energy Commission.

Rabi, Isador I.
A consultant to Oppenheimer at Los Alamos; won the 1944 Nobel Prize for Physics for developing the molecular-beam magnetic-resonance method; served on the general advisory committee of the Atomic Energy Commission.

Segré, Emilio
Italian-born American physicist shared the 1959 Nobel Prize for Physics with Chamberlain for their discovery of the antiproton.

Smith, Cyril
Associate leader of the Chemistry-Metallurgy Division at Los Alamos and later became professor of metallurgy and founding director of the Institute for the Study of Metals at the University of Chicago.

Teller, Edward
Co-signer with Eugene Szilard and Albert Einstein of the 1939 letter to President Roosevelt warning of German development of the atom bomb; began formulating theory for the hydrogen bomb while at Los Alamos and became the leading proponent of its development.

Wilson, Robert
Directed experiments on the Los Alamos cyclotron and was leader of the Experimental Nuclear Physics Division; later became the first director of Fermi National Accelerator Laboratory.

Index of Names

About the Author

Bernice Bidwell Brode (1901-1989) was born in Batavia, New York and moved with her family to Pasadena, California in 1912. She attended Occidental College and University of California's southern branch (now UCLA) and in 1926 married Bob Brode, among the first crop of physicists to take their PhDs at the California Institute of Technology. While her husband taught at the University of California in Berkeley, Bernice earned her bachelor's and master's degrees and produced their two sons, Bill and Jack. During this period, Bernice shared her husband's fellowships and visiting positions at Princeton, London, Cambridge, Manchester, and in Washington D.C. It was there, during World War II, that J. Robert Oppenheimer launched the Brodes on their remarkable adventure by inviting them to join the secret project at Los Alamos

After the war, the Brodes returned to Berkeley where Bob resumed his professorial duties and both participated actively in University affairs. A frequent traveler abroad, Bernice served as assistant to the director of the University of California's Education Abroad Program during an extended residence in London.

Bob died in Berkeley in 1986 and Bernice died in 1989.